D0850520

A COLOURED KEY TO THE WILDFOWL OF THE WORLD

A

COLOURED KEY

TO THE

WILDFOWL

OF THE WORLD

by

PETER SCOTT

THE WILDFOWL TRUST

A Key to the Wildfowl of the World, containing black and white drawings only, was first published in the 2nd Annual Report of the Severn Wildfowl Trust, 1948-49. It was reprinted as a separate book in 1950, revised and reprinted again in 1951.

This coloured version first published in 1957 amounts to an entirely new publication. Substantial additions have been made to the text and there has been further extensive revision in the light of the most recent taxonomic opinion.

Revised and reprinted 1961.
Further revision, 1965, 1968.
Further revision, 1972.

Hardback Edition Printed and Published in Great Britain by W. R. Royle and Son Limited, London N1 7ST, and distributed by H. F. & G. Witherby Ltd.

SBN 85493 013 2

CONTENTS

		PAGE
INTRODUCTION	.. ..	7
KEY	.. ..	9
NAMES AND CLASSIFICATION	.. ..	27
COLOUR PLATES (with systematic list on facing pages)	.. ..	33

	PLATE
Magpie Goose and Whistling Ducks ..	1
Swans	2
Grey Geese	3
Snow Geese	4
Black Geese	5
Shelducks	6
Sheldgeese	7
Cape Barren Goose, Steamer Ducks and Crested Ducks	8
Surface-feeding or Dabbling Ducks, Teal and Pintails	9, 10
Mallards	11
Gadwall, Wigeon, Blue-winged Teal and Shovelers	12
Aberrant species of Dabbling Ducks ..	13
Torrent Ducks	14
Eiders	15
Pochards 16, 17
Perching Ducks and Geese 18, 19
Scoters	20
Harlequins, Longtail and Goldeneyes ..	21
Mergansers or Sawbills	22
Stiff-tails	23

| INDEX OF SCIENTIFIC NAMES | .. .. | 81 |
| INDEX OF ENGLISH NAMES | .. .. | 87 |

ACKNOWLEDGEMENT

I am grateful to Hugh Boyd for help in the revision of the notes on distribution and in compiling the introductory Key and the index.

INTRODUCTION

In this Key there is a coloured picture of every kind of duck, goose or swan so far known to exist in the world—247 kinds. The object of the book is to enable anyone, even without previous experience, to identify any bird within this group (called the family *Anatidae*) which they may see, and to discover its geographical range. It assumes that the bird has been seen at reasonably close quarters on the ground or on the water. The illustrations mainly show the birds in full breeding plumage. From June until October the drakes of many of the species of ducks from the Northern Hemisphere go into a dull "eclipse plumage", which includes the period when the flight feathers are moulted and the birds are flightless. In this eclipse plumage the male in most cases looks very much like the female. The appearance of the females shows no striking change during the year, although it is sometimes affected by wear and tear of the feathers.

Where only one bird is shown as representative of each kind, as in the swans, geese, whistling ducks, etc., the sexes are virtually the same in plumage or, as in certain species of ducks, very similar but with the females slightly duller. In a few cases the female is so similar to that of a closely allied race that she is omitted in order to save space.

In the Key that follows and against the birds in the plates the conventional signs have been used to indicate sex, thus:

    ♂ = male   ♀ = female

    ♂♂ = males   ♀♀ = females

7

HOW TO USE THIS KEY

Each plate shows a group of species which are regarded as being particularly closely related so that in general the birds most likely to be confused with one another are shown on the same page. As a quick guide a certain number of basic characters such as size, shape, colour, behaviour and voice may give a clue to the page you want.

See, first of all, whether you can allocate the bird you are trying to identify to one or more of the headings on the following pages, and then see if you can trace it to a particular plate. Once you have the right plate there *should* be no great difficulty in making a final identification.

RELATIVE SIZES

VERY SMALL
Hottentot Teal

SMALL
Cape Teal

MEDIUM-SIZED
Mallard

RATHER LARGE
Shelduck

VERY LARGE
Whistling Swan

LARGE
Greylag Goose

1. SIZE

Plate No.

Very Large. *Swans* (white, or white with black head and neck, or black; young grey or light brown)..   2

Large races of *Canada Goose* (brown with black head and neck and white cheeks)   5

Spur-winged Goose ♂ ♂ (black and white; rather ugly)   19

Black-necked Swan

Large. *True Geese* (*"Black Geese", "Grey Geese", Snow Geese, Emperor and Barhead*) 3, 4, 5

Sheldgeese (long legs; upright stance) and *Steamer Ducks* (heavy bills) 6, 7, 8

Magpie Goose (black and white; untidy-looking)   1

White-winged Wood Duck, Muscovy Duck (long body, short legs)   19

Comb Duck ♂ ♂ (black with white head and breast, head spotted with black; comb on bill) ..   19

Spur-winged Goose ♀ ♀ (black and white)   ..   19

Muscovy Duck

Plate No.

Rather Large. *Cuban Whistling Duck* (long legs, spotted flanks; rather dark)   1

Shelducks and Sheldgeese (long legs, upright stance) 6, 7

Andean Crested Duck (short legs, long body and tail; brown, with small crest at back of neck)   8

Eiders (thick-set, with massive bills; females brown, males black and white with light green on heads)   15

Goosander ♂ ♂ (long, thin red bill hooked at tip; largely white body, head black; dive often)   22

Goosander ♀ ♀ (long, thin, reddish bill, grey body, brown head with crest at back; dive often)   22

Musk Duck (sooty-black, very broad; male with lobe hanging from bill)   23

Eider

Very Small. *Hottentot Teal* (black crown, cream cheeks with dark patch; bluish bill)   9

Ringed Teal (♂ breast pink, flanks blue-grey, chestnut on sides of back)   13

Brazilian Teal (brown with coral red legs and feet; glossy green wings marked with black and white)   18

Pygmy 'Geese' (tiny goose-like bills, very short legs; backs black glossed with green)   18

Bufflehead (high crowned; largely white beneath, white patch on head; male cheeks glossed green and purple; dives often)   21

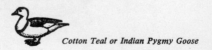

Cotton Teal or Indian Pygmy Goose

Small. *Lesser Whistling Duck* (long legs; brown with blue-grey sheen on back)   1

Teals (some males brightly-coloured, especially on head; females brown) 9, 10, 12, 18

Pink-eared Duck (soft buff and brown; huge bill with flaps at tip   13

Small *Mallards,* i.e., *Hawaiian Duck, Laysan Teal* (undistinguished)   11

Smew (thin pointed bills; male almost white, female grey with brown head, dives often) ..   22

Hooded Merganser (thin pointed bill, male black and white, female brownish; conspicuous flattened crest; dives often)   22

Stifftails (very short and very wide; tail held flat in water or cocked right up; dive often) ..   23

Ruddy Duck

Medium. All the rest.

Pintail

2. SHAPE

Plate No.

Long Neck. *Swans* (white, or white with black head
and neck, or black; young grey or light brown)   2
Magpie Goose (black and white; legs orange-
yellow, bill dirty yellowish; feet scarcely webbed) 1
Spur-winged Goose (black and white; legs flesh,
bill dark red) 19
Pink-headed Duck (probably extinct) 13

Long Legs. *Whistling Ducks* (noisy, sociable, addicted
to perching on trees and posts) 1
Hawaiian Goose (brownish-grey with buff neck
and black head; feet only partially webbed) .. 5
Orinoco Goose (fawn and brown, dark wings,
cherry-red legs; 'wind-swept' neck; very upright
stance) 6
Sheldgeese (rather large; upright stance, small
bills; most forms finely barred black on sides
and breast).. 7
Cape Barren Goose (large; grey, with green bill,
pink legs and black feet; grunts like a pig) .. 8
Spur-winged Goose (very large; black and white;
dark red bill and legs) 19

Elongated Body. *Black-necked Swan* (very large; white
with black head and neck; bright red knob on
bill).. 2
Crested Ducks (rather large; spotty brown;
long black tail, inconspicuous crest at back of
head 8
African Black Ducks (medium-sized; dark
brown; black backs with white spots) 11
*Hartlaub's, Muscovy and White-winged Wood
Ducks* (large or rather large; short legs).. .. 19
Sawbills (long, thin bills; mostly black and white
or brown and grey) 22
Torrent Ducks (pointed bills; upright stance;
long tails) 14

Short Rounded Body. *Eiders* (rather large; females brown; males black and white with brightly-coloured heads and necks) 15
Goldeneyes and Bufflehead (medium-sized and very small; males, black and white females dark brown heads, dive often) 21
Stifftails (mostly rather small, with broad bills; spiky tails carried flat on water or cocked well up; dive often 23

Long Tail. *Crested Ducks* (rather large; mottled brown) 8
Pintails and Salvadori's Duck (medium-sized or rather small) 9
Torrent Ducks (medium-sized; tail broad as well as long; upright stance) 14
Long-tailed Duck ♂ (medium-sized; black and white) 21
Stifftails (mostly rather small; dive often) .. 23

Crest at back of head. *Tufted Duck* ♂ (black and white; dives freely) 17

Tufted Duck

Falcated Duck ♂ (iridescent bronze head) .. 10

Falcated Duck

Mandarin and *Carolina Ducks* (males with larger crests, and very brightly coloured) 18

Mandarin

Carolina or Wood Duck

Crested Shelduck (rather large; long legs; probably extinct) 6

Crested Shelduck

Crested Ducks (rather large; long tail; mottled brown) 8

Crested Duck

13

Plate No.

Marbled Teal (small; beige-coloured with soft black spots; crest inconspicuous) 9

Marbled Teal

Mergansers (long thin bills) 22

Red-breasted Merganser

Hooded Merganser

Goosander ♀ ♀ (long thin bills; chestnut heads) 22

Smew ♂ (nearly white) 22

Smew

Tuft on crown. *Red-crested Pochard* ♂ (crown orange, like shaving-brush) 16

Cuban and Spotted Whistling Ducks (long legs; flanks spotted with white; tuft inconspicuous) .. 1

Red-crested Pochard

3. BILL SHAPE

Long thin bill, hooked at tip. *Goosander, Merganser* and *Smew* (Sawbills) 22

Goosander ♂

Torrent Ducks (bills bright red) 14

Torrent Duck

Long, broad, spoonshaped. *Shovelers* (medium-sized) 12

Shoveler

Long with flaps at tip. *Pink-eared Duck* (small; light brownish-grey with fine black bars) 13

Pink-eared Duck

Making straight line with forehead. *Swans* (very large) 2

Swan Goose (large, with black bill and dark brown stripe down back of neck) 3

Swan Goose

Eiders (rather large; males black and white with coloured heads, females brown) 15

Canvasback (medium-sized – larger than *Pochard* or *Redhead;* dives often) 16

Eider

Comb or Knob above bill. *Mute Swan* (very large; white; orange-pink bill; knob black) 2

Black-necked Swan (white with black head and neck; knob red) 2

Domestic Chinese Goose (large; upright stance, imperious look; belly nearly touches ground) .. 3

Comb Duck or Knob-nosed Goose ♂ (rather large; white head with black spots; knob black) 19

Comb Duck

Muscovy Duck ♂ (large; black glossed with green. Domestic forms white, grey or black, or mixtures; knob black or red) 19

Rosybill ♂ (medium-sized; black and grey with cherry-red bill) 16

Some *Scoter* ♂ ♂ (medium-sized; glossy black) 20

White-headed Stifftail ♂ (bill blue; dives often) 23

King Eider ♂ (medium-sized; black with pink breast, blue-grey head; knob orange) 15

King Eider

Lobe hanging under bill. *Musk Duck* ♂ (rather large; sooty dark grey; dives often) 23

Musk Duck

Down-curved bill. *Blue Duck* (medium-sized; grey, with flesh-coloured bill) 13

Blue Duck

Cape Barren Goose (large; grey, with greenish bill) 8

Cape Barren Goose

Very large, heavy bill. *Steamer Ducks* (large; grey marked with brown) 8

Steamer Duck

Thick-billed Bean Goose (large; brownish-grey, orange band on bill and orange legs) 3

Thick-billed Bean Goose *Eastern Greylag Goose* (large; pale brownish-grey, bill and legs pink) 3

4. COLOUR

Very Bright with complex pattern.

Red-breasted Goose (medium-sized; black, sharply marked with chestnut and white) .. 5

Baikal Teal ♂ (small, with black, green, buff and white on head) 10

Mandarin Duck ♂ (medium-sized, with orange hackles and 'sails', white stripe on head) .. 18

Carolina or *Wood Duck* ♂ (medium-sized, with glossy green and white head, purple breast, scarlet eye, orange bill) 18

African Pygmy Goose ♂ (small; chestnut breast and flanks, green patch on side of head; bright orange bill) 18

King Eider ♂ (medium-sized; black and white, with pink breast, blue-grey and pale green patches on head, orange-red bill) 15

Steller's Eider ♂ (small; black and white, chestnut below shading to orange-pink, green patches on head) 15

Harlequin Duck ♂ (medium-sized; blue-grey and white with chestnut flanks and sandy-orange stripe over eye) 21

White. *Swans* (very large; long-necked) 2

Snow Geese (large; pink bill and legs; black wing-tips) 4

Kelp Goose ♂ (large; black bill and yellow legs; all plumage pure white) 7

Nearly White. *Magellan or Upland Geese* ♂ ♂ (large;
upright stance; barred flanks, grey backs) .. 7
Smew (small; white, with some black markings
on head and back; thin, rather pointed bill) .. 22
Immatures of *Swans, Snow Geese* and *Kelp
Geese* 2, 4, 7

Black. *Black Swan* (very large; long-necked, with white
wing-tips) 2
Muscovy Duck (large; short-legged; black with
green or purple gloss, white patch on wing) .. 19
Scoter ♂ ♂ (medium-sized ducks, black with
coloured bill) 20
N.Z. Shelduck ♂ (rather large; long-legged, with
green and white in wing) 6

Sharply Black-and-White. *Black-necked Swan* (very
large; white, with black neck) 2
Magpie Goose (large; white with black head,
neck and wings) 1
Common Shelduck (rather large; white with
black head, neck and wings, chestnut band on
breast; red bill) 6
Goosander ♂ ♂ (rather large; white, with black
head and back; long hook-tipped bill) 22
Eider ♂ ♂ (rather large; with white shoulders,
white or pink breast, black body, green patches
on head) 15
Tufted and *Ring-necked Duck* ♂ ♂ (medium-
sized diving ducks with black heads, necks and
bodies, white or pale grey sides).. 17
Common and *Barrow's Goldeneye* ♂ ♂ (medium-
sized diving ducks with black heads, white
breasts, flanks and some white on the back;
white spot in front of eye) 21

Chestnut. *Ruddy Shelduck* (rather large; nearly uni-
formly coloured, with paler head, black tail and
wing tips) 6

Cape Shelduck (rather large; chestnut bodies, grey or grey and white head, black tail and wing tips) 6

Hartlaub's Duck (medium-sized; dark chestnut with black or black and white head; blue in wing) 19

Cinnamon Teal ♂ ♂ (small; blue in wing usually hidden when at rest) 12

Stifftail ♂ ♂ (small; round; head black or black and white; blue bill) 23

Pink Head. *Pink-headed Duck* (medium-sized; long pink neck and head, dark brown body. May now be extinct) 13

Orange Head. *Red-crested Pochard* ♂ (medium-sized; orange head and crest, red bill) 16

5. BRIGHTLY-COLOURED BILLS

Red Bill. *Coscoroba* (very large white bird) 2

Black Swan (very large black bird) 2

Spur-winged Goose (very large black and white bird with long legs) 19

Common Shelduck (rather large duck; bill broad) 6

Goosander (rather large duck; bill long and pointed, or with hooked tip) 22

Red-crested Pochard ♂ (medium-sized duck with orange head, brown in eclipse) 16

Rosybill ♂ (medium-sized duck with black head and neck) 16

Red-billed Pintail (medium-sized duck with brown body, pale cheeks) 9

Red-billed Whistling Duck (medium-sized duck with brown body, black belly, long legs) .. 1

Torrent Ducks (medium-sized; males with black and white patterned heads, long tails, females grey above, chestnut below) 14

Brazilian and Schuyl's Teal (small and medium-sized brownish-grey duck, with dazzling red legs) 18

Mandarin Duck ♂ (medium-sized duck with orange hackles and 'sails', white stripe on head)   18

Red spot on bill. *Bahama Pintail* (warm brown with dark crown and white cheeks; bill blue with red spot at base)   9

Indian and *Burma Spotbills* (pale mallards with white in wing; yellow tip to bill and red spot at base)   11

Orange Bill. *Pacific, Northern* or *King Eider* ♂ ♂ (rather large black and white duck)   15

White-winged Wood Duck (rather large; blackish-brown with spotty white head and spotty bill) ..   19

African Pygmy Goose (small duck, dark green above and chestnut on breast and flanks)   ..   18

Western Greylag Goose (large brownish-grey bird with pinkish legs)   3

Bean Geese (large brownish-grey birds with orange legs and some black on bill)   3

Carolina or *Wood Duck* ♂ (medium-sized duck with glossy green and white head, purple breast, scarlet eye)   18

Yellow Bill. *Magpie Goose* (large black and white; bill variously covered with dark scaly spots)   ..   1

Bar-headed Goose (large pale grey goose with black bars over head)   4

Spectacled Eider ♂ (rather large black and white duck with pale green on head)   15

Greenland Whitefront (rather large dark brown goose with white forehead and orange legs)   ..   3

Abyssinian and *African Yellowbills* (medium-sized dark brown mottled ducks with black stripe down centre of bright yellow bill)   11

Green Bill. *Cape Barren Goose* (large grey goose with green top to bill)   8

European, American or *Faeroe Eider* (rather large ducks, with long, high bills) 15

Mallard ♂ ♂ (glossy green heads, maroon breasts, or plain brown with spots in some races) .. 11

Blue Bill. *Stifftail* or *Ruddy Duck* ♂ ♂ (small diving ducks, round in shape with chestnut bodies, black heads with or without white cheeks) .. 23

Puna Teal (medium-sized grey duck with black crown and white cheeks; black line along centre of bill) 9

Silver Teal (small grey teal with black crown, cream cheeks; black line along centre of bill and yellow spot at base in ♂, sometimes in ♀) .. 9

Hottentot Teal (very small brownish duck with black crown, cream cheeks with a dark patch).. 9

Ringed Teal ♂ (very small duck with creamy grey cheeks, pink breast, chestnut on sides of back).. 13

Philippine Duck (medium-sized grey duck with light chestnut face and sharp eye-stripe) .. 11

Bahama and *Galapagos Pintails* (medium or small; brown; white cheeks, red spot at base of bill) 9

Black-necked Swan (very large white bird with black head and neck and red knob above blue bill) 2

Red-breasted Goose

6. VOICE

Trumpeting or bugling. *Trumpeter, Whooper, Whistling* and *Bewick's Swans* (very large white birds) 2

Honking. *True Geese* (very large or large birds; brown-, or grey-, or black-and-white, or white) 3, 4, 5

White-winged Wood Duck ♀ (large, blackish duck, dark brown breast, spotted white head and white in wing) 19

Magpie Goose (large, black-and-white, with long orange-yellow legs) 1

Shelducks (rather large, brightly-coloured, with varying amounts of chestnut or orange-brown on body) 6

Whistling. *Whistling Ducks* (long-legged birds with an upright stance) 1

Common Shelduck ♂ (rather large, black-and-white, with red knobbed bill and red-brown band on breast) 6

Radjah Shelduck ♂ (medium-sized, white with pale pink bill and brown back) 6

Sheldgeese ♂ ♂ (large; white, black-and-white, or brown with black-barred flanks) 7

Northern Pintail ♂ (medium-sized, with very pointed tail and slender neck) 9

Green-winged, Chilean and *Sharp-winged Teal* ♂ ♂ (small ducks) 9

Wigeon ♂ ♂ (medium-sized ducks with white or buff crowns) 12

Ringed Teal ♂ (very small, with creamy-grey face, blue bill, pink breast, blue-grey sides) .. 13

Blue Duck ♂ (medium-sized blue-grey duck with odd bill 'flanged' near the tip) 13

Pink-eared Duck ♂ (small duck; huge bill with flaps at tip).. 13

White-backed Duck (small brownish duck with barred sides and short tail) 23

Barking. *Sheldgeese* ♀ ♀ (large; white with red legs or mainly brown with yellow legs) 7

Cape Barren Goose ♂ (large, grey, with green bill, pink legs and black feet) 8

Bronze-winged Duck ♀ (medium-sized brown duck with white crescent on face and white throat pattern) 9

Goosander ♀ (medium-sized, grey and white, with long pointed red bill, hooked at tip, and red-brown crested head) 22

Quacking. *Dabbling Duck* ♀ ♀ (medium-sized or small, mainly brown) 9, 10, 11, 12

Clucking. *Baikal Teal* ♂ (small, with bronze-green and buff patterning on head) 10
Shoveler ♂ (small, with very large bill) .. 12

Rattling or nattering. *Radjah Shelduck* ♀ (medium-sized, white, with pale pink bill and legs, reddish brown or dark brown on back) 6
Crested Duck ♀ (rather large mottled brown with long tail and a small crest) 8
Bronze-winged Duck ♀ (medium-sized, brown, with white crescent on face and white patch under chin) 9
Garganey ♂ (small, white stripe above eye, brown head, pale grey flanks, greyish back; sounds like fishing reel) 12
Blue-winged Teal ♂ (small; mottled red-brown, grey head with white crescent on side of face) .. 12
Cinnamon Teal ♂ (small, deep chestnut, with sky-blue shoulders [usually hidden]) 12
Smew ♂ (small white bird with black markings on head and back, thin, sharp bill) 22

Grunting. *Cape Barren Goose* ♀ (large, grey, with green bill, pink legs and black feet) 8
Gadwall ♂ (medium-sized grey and brown duck with black under tail) 12

Laughing. *Common Shelduck* ♀ (rather large, black and white, red bill, red-brown band across breast) 6

Plate No.

Hissing. *Mute Swan* (very large, white, orange and black bill) 2

Egyptian Goose ♂ (large grey bird with chestnut brown markings, including patch round yellow eye) 6

Muscovy Duck ♂ (large black duck with black or red lumpy bill; sounds like small steam engine) 19

True Geese (in defence) 3, 4, 5

7. BEHAVIOUR

Frequent Diving. *Torrent Ducks* (medium-sized, slim build, with long stiff tails, red bills and feet) .. 14

Pochards (medium-sized, ♂ ♂ smartly marked, females brown) 16, 17

Male Goldeneye

Eiders (rather large, or medium-sized; ♂ ♂ black and white with coloured heads, ♀ ♀ brown; both sexes with large bills) 15

Scoters (medium-sized; ♂ ♂ black, ♀ ♀ brown) 20

Harlequins, Longtail and *Goldeneyes* (medium-sized or smaller, mostly black- or brown-and-white) 21

Sawbills (black-and-white or grey-and-white, with long thin, pointed or hooked bills) .. 22

Stifftails (small or very small, 'tubby'; ♂ ♂ chestnut, black and white, with blue bills, ♀ ♀ brown) 23

Whistling Ducks (sometimes) (medium-sized or small, with long legs and necks) 1

Grazing. *Swans* (very large white or black and white birds) 2

True Geese (very large or large; brown-, or grey-, or black-and-white, or white) 3, 4, 5

Red-breasted Goose

Sheldgeese (large, long-legged, with small bills; white or brown, with black barring on flanks, and sometimes on breast) 7

Wigeon (medium-sized ducks; ♂ ♂ brightly-coloured with white or buff crowns, ♀ ♀ duller) 12

23

Australian Wood Duck (♂ grey with chocolate head, ♀ mottled grey and brown) 18

Perching on branches, posts, etc. *Magpie Goose*
(large; black and white, orange yellowlegs and bill) 1

Whistling Ducks (medium-sized or small, long legs, upright stance) 1

Radjah Shelduck (medium-sized; white with pink bill and feet, dark brown back and breast band) 6

Red-billed
Whistling Duck

Orinoco Goose (very upright; neck 'wind-swept'; fawn, with chestnut flanks, greenish-black wings, cherry-red legs) 6

Green-winged Teal (small; ♂ ♂ with brown and green head and grey-brown body; ♀ ♀ brown) 9

White-winged Wood and *Muscovy Duck* (large; rather ugly; black with white patches) 19

Spur-winged Goose (very large; very ugly; black and white, with dark red bill and legs) 19

Mutual Preening. *White-faced Whistling Duck* (rather
small; long-legged, upright stance) 1

Orinoco Goose (rather large, upright stance; fawn with chestnut flanks, greenish-black wings and cherry-red legs) 6

Mandarin and *Carolina Ducks* (small; ♂ ♂ improbably and brilliantly coloured with crests, ♀ ♀ greyish-brown, mottled underneath) 18

White-faced Whistling Ducks

IF YOU ARE STUCK

If you are unable to identify your bird from the Key or from the Plates the following possibilities should then be carefully considered.

The bird may be:

1. An immature specimen, the plumage of which is likely to be similar to the female, or intermediate between that of the male and female.

2. A male in eclipse plumage of one of the species in which the drake spends several months in a dull plumage usually resembling the female. Intermediate plumages occur during the transition.

3. A hybrid. These are comparatively frequent in wildfowl and the parentage is not always apparent even to an expert eye.

4. A variety or freak, showing white in patches (schizochromism) or a uniform paleness of plumage (leucism) or blackness (melanism). Pure albinism – pure white with pink eyes – has very rarely been recorded in wildfowl.

5. Descended from domestic stock. Such birds, capable of flight, include some tame grey or white or 'skewbald' geese (from Greylag stock) and Chinese Geese (Plate 3). Much more frequently mistaken for wild birds, however, are various forms of the Mallard (Plate 11) which show domestic blood and the domestic form of the Muscovy Duck (Plate 18), all of which may be quite good fliers.

   Mallards showing domestic blood may take the following forms:

   (i) White Call Ducks (small; white with yellow or orange bill)

   (ii) Cayuga Ducks (medium-sized; black or dark reddish-brown, with black head and variable-sized white patch on breast.)[1]

---

[1] It has not yet been established whether these birds, which are not uncommon, are descended from domestic 'Cayuga' type stock or whether they represent a fairly frequent mutation capable of arising from perfectly wild stock.

(iii) Mallards with white wing-tips, broad white neck-rings, etc.

Muscovy Ducks with domestic blood can be:

(iv) Black glossed with green; white in wings; variable additional white, most often on head; bill swollen and bright red or black and red.

(v) Pure white with red bill.

(vi) Pale grey, usually with white head and red bill.

(vii) Mixtures of all three colours.

If you have seen a striking duck or goose which you cannot trace from this Key or from the Plates, it is very likely to be a Muscovy Duck, or a Mallard showing domestic blood, or a hybrid – in that order of probability.

Domestic Muscovy Duck

Mallard of 'Cayuga' type

Hybrid Mallard × Pintail Male

26

NAMES AND CLASSIFICATION

All the birds in this book are given at least two names. Those printed in bold type are the English, or vernacular, names. The choice of these names is not governed by strict rules of procedure and people differ more or less strongly in their preferences. The ones used here are for the most part those in general use in ornithological handbooks. For species found in Britain these are the same as the 'common' names, used by wildfowlers and birdwatchers and those with just a general interest in the birds around them. But the textbook names given to species occurring elsewhere, in Australia for example, do not necessarily coincide with the names used locally. This Key tries to include the most widely-used of such local names, though confining itself to English ones.

The names printed in italic type are those applied to the different kinds of birds according to the formal procedure of taxonomy. It may be helpful to explain briefly the significance and use of such names. Taxonomy, the study of the principles of classification of animals (and plants), has two distinct components, classification and nomenclature. *Classification* deals with the ranking of various categories (such as family, genus, species) to which organisms are assigned in accordance with their evolutionary relationships, and *nomenclature* deals with the legalistic aspect of names (which name should properly be used for a given animal, according to the International Code of Zoological Nomenclature).

Classification has a double purpose. From a practical point of view, a system of grouping makes it easier to identify animals. From a theoretical point of view a "natural" classification shows, to some extent, the relationships or supposed relationships of the groups concerned and helps to indicate the course which evolution has taken.

The system of classification applied to animals may best be demonstrated by means of examples taken from the text opposite Plate 1. The groups used are in a hierarchy, in which any category includes all the subsequent (lower) categories. The six universally recognised categories, in descending order of rank, are: Phylum, Class, Order, Family, Genus and Species.

This system is expanded according to the needs of specialists in any group by using the prefixes "super-" and "sub-". Birds belong to the Phylum *Chordata* (which includes all vertebrate animals and those animals without vertebrae which possess a notochord) and form the Class *Aves*. The swans, geese and ducks are included in the Order *Anseriformes,* one of twenty-three orders into which the Class *Aves* is divided. The Order *Anseriformes* includes the Family *Anhimidae* (the Screamers) and the family *Anatidae*. (Swans, geese and ducks.)[1]

The Family *Anatidae* is divided into three Sub-Families. The Magpie Goose (Plate 1) is considered so different from all other wildfowl in the details of its anatomy that it is assigned to the Sub-Family *Anseranatinae* while the remainder are assigned to the Sub-Families *Anserinae* (Swans, Geese and Whistling Ducks) or *Anatinae* (the remaining ducks). Delacour and Mayr, whose paper *The Family Anatidae* (Wilson Bulletin Vol. 57, No. 1, pp. 3–55, 1945) provides the basis of the classification adopted in this Key, insert a further category, the Tribe, between the Sub-Family and the Genus. They use the term tribe (with the ending *-ini*) for a recognisable group of genera within each sub-family. The Magpie Goose forms a Tribe, a genus and a species by itself.

The Sub-Family *Anserinae* is divided by Delacour and Mayr into two tribes, *Anserini* – the Swans and Geese, and *Dendrocygnini* – the Whistling Ducks (Plate 1). All the members of the Tribe *Dendrocygnini* are assigned to a single Genus, *Dendrocygna*. But the Tribe *Anserini* includes four genera, *Coscoroba, Cygnus, Anser* and *Branta,* while the Sub-Family *Anatinae* is divided into seven tribes and includes 34 genera.

This lack of numerical equivalence between the groups shows the complexity of the relationships within the Family. But though it is difficult to give any precise meaning to the concepts, there is a general belief that genera and above all species form comparable natural units, whether in birds or mammals, or invertebrates or plants. The scientific name of the Magpie Goose is made up of the generic name *Anseranas*

---

[1] Some consider that the Family *Phœnicopteridae* (the Flamingos) should also be included in the order *Anseriformes*.

(Goose-duck) and the specific name *semipalmata* (half-webbed). This use of the combination of generic and specific names to describe the most important recognisable natural group – the species – is the principle of binomial nomenclature, first consistently applied by the great Swedish taxonomist Linnaeus in the middle of the eighteenth century.

All these long Latin names are subject to a strict set of rules of nomenclature. Only the method of choosing the generic and specific names will be illustrated here, although rules are also laid down for applying the correct names to higher groups. The first principle of naming a species is that a type specimen of the organism shall be described under that name. The desscription must be detailed enough to make clear what differences are supposed to exist between the named specimens and other rather similar animals, and the species must be provided with a type locality, wherever possible the place at which the type specimen was collected. It has frequently happened that someone has described an animal as of a new species only for it to be shown later that a similar animal had been described earlier by someone else, so that two (or more) names are available for the same species. To get over this difficulty there is a rule of priority. The first specific name applied to a species must stand, except in very special circumstances, which have to be argued for any particular case.

The generic name consists of a single word, printed with an initial capital. The specific name is also a single word, written with a small initial letter. These, and all scientific names, must be words which are either Latin or latinized or are treated as such in case they are not of classic origin. The original describer can choose what specific name he likes, providing it agrees grammatically with the generic name. Usually the names chosen refer to a feature of the bird's appearance, or where it lives, though sometimes the describer names an animal in honour of a friend, or another specialist in the same group, or the collector who obtained the type specimen.

Three words in a scientific name indicate that the species seems to be made up of several more or less distinct groups, separated geographically, which though sufficiently alike to

29

justify them being regarded as a single species, show sufficient variation from group to group to enable most individuals to be identifiable as members of one subspecies rather than another. (Subspecies are sometimes referred to as 'races' and as 'forms', and in this context the three terms are almost synonymous, though 'form' would also include species which are not subdivided into subspecies or races.) One of the subspecies repeats the specific name, while the remainder are given additional names. Some examples may make this clearer.

The Whistling Ducks of Plate 1 illustrate all these points. The Spotted Whistling Duck is called *Dendrocygna guttata*. *Dendrocygna* means "tree-swan" – a reference to the long-necked appearance of all members of the genus, and to their habit of perching on trees – and *guttata* means spotted. *Dendrocygna eytoni* is named for the man who discovered and described the species. (It is not now usual for a taxonomist to name a species after himself.) Both these species show no signs of geographical variation. But the Wandering Whistling Duck *Dendrocygna arcuata* (the specific name *arcuata,* arched or bowed, refers to the flank feathers) forms three geographical races or subspecies. The Wandering Whistling Ducks of the East Indies form one subspecies. Since the type specimen of the species came from this area this subspecies must be called *Dendrocygna arcuata arcuata*. Australian specimens are larger and can be recognised as *Dendrocygna arcuata australis,* while specimens from New Britain, which are a good deal smaller, are distinguishable as *D.a. pygmœa*. (When generic and specific names need to be referred to repeatedly they can be contracted to their initial letters for brevity.) You will notice in the text that it is uncertain to which race birds from New Caledonia should be allotted. This kind of overlap is frequently found. Sometimes fuller investigation enables a clear-cut decision to be made, but often it must be accepted that such birds are truly intermediate, in which case, though the forms at each end of the varying population are given distinct names, the intermediate birds cannot be given a tri-nominal name and may be treated as *D.a. australis ⪦ pygmœa* or in some other inevitably clumsy way.

It will be noted that another name in Roman type follows the specific or subspecific name, e.g., *Dendrocygna guttata* Schlagel. This is the author's name. The author of a scientific name is the person who first publishes the name in connection with a description. The author's name is not always given as part of the scientific name, but is useful in making clear which type description is being used in cases where the history of the name is complicated. (There are uncomfortably many complications, because most names originate from 150 to 200 years ago, a period when first publications were often in obscure journals not widely circulated, so that species were often described as "new" several times by different authors in the course of a few years.) Changing ideas about relationships have also caused the accepted limits of many species to vary. Changing ideas about relationships are responsible too for the presence or absence of parentheses enclosing the author's name. The rule is that the author's name appears without brackets if he originally described the species as a member of the genus in which it is now placed. But if the author placed it in another genus, then his name appears in brackets. For example, Eyton first described the Plumed Whistling Duck (in 1838) under the name *Leptotarsis eytoni*. Since it is now considered to belong to the genus *Dendrocygna, Leptotarsis eytoni* Eyton has been replaced by *Dendrocygna eytoni* (Eyton).

The contractions L. or (L.) which appear frequently instead of an author's name stand for Linneaus, the inaugurator of binomial nomenclature.

The 247 forms of swans, geese and ducks – all that are so far known to science – are comprised within 151 full species. Of these 51 forms (of 45 species) have been found in a wild state in Britain and three more, originally introduced as captives, have now formed feral free-living populations (the Canada Goose, Egyptian Goose and Mandarin Duck). These 54 forms are marked in the text thus *. Four species and two races believed to have become altogether extinct throughout the world within recent years are marked thus †.

31

SCALE OF THE PLATES

It should be noticed that five different scales have been used in the drawings—one for the swans (Plate 2), one for the True Geese and Sheldgeese (Plates 3, 4, 5, 7), one for the Shelducks and Perching Geese (Plates 6, 18), one for the Whistling Ducks, Crested and Steamer Ducks and Cape Barren Goose, and Scoters (Plates 1, 8, 20) and one for the rest of the ducks (Plates 9–17, 19, 21–23). This complication has arisen because, within the framework of the natural groupings, the birds have been drawn as large as possible in order to show the detail; teal would be too small to show the markings if drawn on the same scale as swans, all of which must be shown on one page.

Salvadori's Duck

PLATE 1

Sub-order ANSERES
Family ANATIDAE
Sub-family ANSERANATINAE
Tribe ANSERANATINI

Magpie Goose. *Anseranas semipalmata* (Latham).
Southern New Guinea and northern Australia, especially Arnhem Land.

Sub-family ANSERINAE
Tribe DENDROCYGNINI (Whistling Ducks or Tree Ducks)

Spotted Whistling Duck. *Dendrocygna guttata* Schlegel.
East Indies (Mindanao, Celebes, Moluccas, Tenimber, Aru, New Guinea, Bismarck Archipelago).

Plumed or **Eyton's Whistling Duck.** *Dendrocygna eytoni* (Eyton).
Australia, including Tasmania, but abundant only in the tropics.

East Indian Wandering Whistling Duck. *Dendrocygna arcuata arcuata* (Horsfield).
East Indies (Borneo, Sumatra, Java, Bali, Sumba, Timor, Celebes, Moluccas and Philippines).

Australian Wandering Whistling Duck. *Dendrocygna arcuata australis* Reichenbach.
Tropical Australia and southern New Guinea. Birds in northern New Guinea (and formerly in New Caledonia) probably belong to this form, or are intermediate between it and *pygmœa*.

Lesser Wandering Whistling Duck. *Dendrocygna arcuata pygmœa* Mayr.
New Britain (and formerly Fiji Islands, where it has probably been exterminated by the introduction of the mongoose).

Fulvous Whistling Duck. *Dendrocygna bicolor* (Vieillot).
South from southern California and Texas to central Mexico; northern tropical South America from Colombia to the Guianas; Brazil, Peru, south to Paraguay and northern Argentina; East Africa from Lake Chad to Natal; Madagascar; India, Ceylon and Burma, south to Pegu. (This is a most extraordinary distribution for any species of bird. There is no geographical variation throughout this huge and broken range).

Black-billed or **Cuban Whistling Duck.** *Dendrocygna arborea* (L.).
West Indies (Bahama Islands, Greater Antilles—Cuba, Haiti, Jamaica, Puerto Rico—Virgin Islands, Leeward Islands, Martinique).

Lesser or **Indian Whistling Duck.** *Dendrocygna javanica* (Horsfield).
India from Sind eastwards to coast of southern China, south to Ceylon, Nicobar Islands, Malay Peninsula, Siam, Cochin China; Riu Kiu Islands, south-western Borneo, Sumatra and Java.

White-faced Whistling Duck. *Dendrocygna viduata* (L.).
Tropical South America, south to the Argentine Chaco, Paraguay and Uruguay. Africa, south of the Sahara to southern Angola and the Transvaal; Madagascar; Comoro Islands.

Northern Red-billed Whistling Duck. *Dendrocygna autumnalis autumnalis* (L.).
Extreme southern Texas and Mexico, south through Central America to Panama, where it intergrades with *D.a. discolor*.

Southern Red-billed Whistling Duck. *Dendrocygna autumnalis discolor* Sclater & Salvin.
South America from eastern Panama to northern Argentina, but not south of Ecuador on the west side of the Andes.

34

Plate 1

MAGPIE GOOSE AND WHISTLING OR TREE DUCKS

Northern Red-billed or Black-bellied Whistling Duck or Tree Duck

The two races intergrade

Magpie, Semi-palmated, or Pied Goose

Male has higher crown than female

Southern Red-billed Whistling Duck or Tree Duck

Black-billed or Cuban Tree Duck

Wandering Tree Ducks East Indian (top of three) *Lesser* (middle) and *Australian* (bottom)

♂ and ♀ have the same plumage in all the forms on this page

Medium

Small

Large

Fulvous Tree Duck or Whistling " Teal "

Javan Tree Duck or Lesser Whistling " Teal "

White-faced Tree Duck

Plumed or Eyton's Tree Duck

Spotted Tree Duck

P.S.

PLATE 2

Tribe ANSERINI (Swans and Geese)

Coscoroba Swan. *Coscoroba coscoroba* (Molina).

Breeds in southern Brazil, Uruguay, Paraguay, Argentina, Chile (including Tierra del Fuego), and Falkland Islands. Winters further north, to about 25°S. This species may more properly belong to the Tribe *Dendrocygnini.*

Black Swan. *Cygnus atratus* (Latham).

Australia, on mainland (except extreme north central) and Tasmania. Introduced into New Zealand, where now widespread.

*Mute Swan. *Cygnus olor* (Gmelin).

Now breeds wild in British Isles, north west Europe, Russia, Asia Minor and Persia, east through Turkestan to Mongolia. In winter to Black Sea, north-western India and Korea. Elsewhere widely introduced.

Black-necked Swan. *Cygnus melanocoryphus* (Molina).

Breeds in South America, from 30°S. in Brazil, Paraguay, Uruguay, Falkland Islands, Argentina and Chile, south to Tierra del Fuego. In winter north to Tropic of Capricorn.

Whistling Swan. *Cygnus columbianus columbianus* (Ord).

North America, breeding chiefly north of Arctic Circle from Alaska to Hudson Bay, and wintering on the Atlantic coast from Chesapeake Bay to Currituck Sound and the Pacific coast from southern Alaska to California.

*Bewick's Swan. *Cygnus columbianus bewickii* Yarrell.

Breeds in northern Russia from the Kanin peninsula and northern Siberia, east to the Lena Delta; south in winter to the British Isles and northern Europe.

Eastern Bewick's or **Jankowski's Swan.** *Cygnus columbianus jankowskii* Alpheraky.

Breeds from the delta of the Lena to the delta of the Kolyma; south to China and Japan in winter. There is some doubt whether this race, which is said to have a larger and more yellow bill, can be shown to be really distinct from *C.c. bewickii.*

*Whooper Swan. *Cygnus cygnus cygnus* (L.).

Breeds from Iceland and northern Scandinavia eastwards to Kamchatka, Commander Islands and Japan. Winters British Isles, western Europe, Asia Minor, northern India, central Asia, China and Japan. Seems formerly to have bred in Greenland, where frequently seen.

Trumpeter Swan. *Cygnus cygnus buccinator* Richardson.

Formerly bred throughout North America. Now known to breed only in Alberta, British Columbia, Montana, Wyoming and interior of Alaska. Population now numbers about 7,000, which represents a considerable increase in recent years.

Plate 2

SWANS

Trumpeter

Whistling **Whooper**

Bewick's **Jankowski's**
The two races
intergrade

In the Swans the plumage of
the male and female (cob and
pen) is the same

Immatures are greyish with
pale flesh-coloured to orange
bills

Slightly
larger,
higher
bill

Trumpeter

Whooper

Whistling
Yellow spot
not always present

Bewick's

Mute

Mute Swan
Adult and Immature
The species which
has become largely
domesticated

*Coscoroba
Swan*

Black Swan

*Black-necked
Swan*

P.S.

PLATE 3

Swan Goose. *Anser cygnoides* (L.).
Breeds in southern Siberia, northern Mongolia and central Manchuria from the Tobol and the Ob to the Sea of Okhotsk and Sakhalin. Winters in China. Domestic varieties of "Chinese Geese" are derived from this species.

*Western or **Yellow-billed Bean Goose.**
Anser fabalis fabalis (Latham).
Breeds in wooded country of the Arctic from Lapland eastwards to the Ural Mountains. Winters in Britain (now very local and less than 300 birds), Holland, Europe south to Mediterranean and Black Seas. Limits of ranges of this and next four races not yet fully determined.

Johansen's Bean Goose. *Anser fabalis johanseni* Delacour.
Breeds in forested western Siberia east to Khatanga and south to about 61°N. Mingles and interbreeds with *rossicus* in the north and intergrades with *fabalis* and *middendorfi* where their ranges are in contact. Winters in Persia, Turkestan and western China.

Middendorf's Bean Goose. *Anser fabalis middendorfi* Severtzow.
Breeds in forests of eastern Siberia from the Khatanga to the Kolyma, south to the Altai. Winters in eastern China, northern Mongolia and Japan.

*Russian Bean Goose. *Anser fabalis rossicus* Buturlin.
Breeds in Novaya Zemlya and on tundra shores of Arctic Russia and Siberia west of the Taimyr Peninsula. Winters in Europe west to Belgium and Holland, south to Italy; in southern Russia, Siberia, Turkestan and China. Individuals stray to Britain. "Sushkin's Goose" appears to be a colour phase of this race, with pink bill and legs.

Thick-billed or **Eastern Bean Goose.** *Anser fabalis serrirostris* Swinhoe.
Breeds on the tundra shores of Siberia, east of the Yenesei. Winters in China and Japan.

*Pink-footed Goose. *Anser brachyrhynchus* Baillon.
Breeds in east Greenland, Iceland and Spitzbergen. Birds from Greenland and Iceland winter in Scotland and England, those from Spitzbergen in Denmark, Germany, Holland, Belgium, occasionally France.

*European White-fronted Goose. *Anser albifrons albifrons* (Scopoli).
Breeds on the Arctic coasts of Europe and Asia, east from the Kanin Peninsula, Kolguev and southern Novaya Zemlya to the Kolyma River and perhaps beyond. Winters in England and Wales, western Europe, on shores of Mediterranean, Black and Caspian Seas, in northern India, China and Japan.

Pacific White-fronted Goose. *Anser albifrons frontalis* Baird.
Breeds in Arctic America, from Mackenzie River west to Bering Sea, and in eastern Siberia, but western limits unknown. Winters in western United States, south to Mexico and east to Louisiana; and in China and Japan.

*Greenland White-fronted Goose. *Anser albifrons flavirostris* Dalgety and Scott.
Breeds in west Greenland. Winters in Ireland, west Scotland, Wales, England (in small numbers); occasional in eastern North America.

Tule Goose. *Anser albifrons gambelli* Hartlaub.
Breeding area unknown, perhaps Victoria Island, off central arctic coast of Canada. Winters very locally in Sacramento Valley, California, in small numbers. White-fronted Geese breeding on the Perry River, on the Canadian mainland south-east of Victoria Island, are intermediate between *gambelli* and *frontalis*.

*Lesser White-fronted Goose. *Anser erythropus* (L.).
Breeds, mostly near mountain tarns, from Norwegian Lapland to the Kolyma in Siberia and perhaps farther eastwards. Winters in south-eastern Europe, Black and Caspian Seas, Turkestan, north-west India, China and Japan. Rare straggler to Britain, occurring almost annually in flocks of White-fronted or Bean Geese.

*Western Greylag Goose. *Anser anser anser* (L.).
Breeds in Scotland, though now only in small numbers. The only indigenous species of goose breeding in Britain. Breeding range includes Iceland, Scandinavia, south to Austria, Yugoslavia, Macedonia and the Caucasus. Winters in Britain, Holland, France, Spain, North Africa. Populations of western Russia and the Balkans are intermediate between this and the Eastern form and further study may reveal more distinguishable populations. The Greylag is the ancestor of domestic geese, other than Chinese.

Eastern Greylag Goose. *Anser anser rubrirostris* Swinhoe.
Breeds eastwards from about 40°E. and south of 60°N. through Asia Minor and central Asia to Kamchatka. In winter to the eastern Mediterranean, Black and Caspian Seas and in Seistan, north-west India and China.

Plate 3

GREY GEESE

The plumage of males and females is the same

Domestic Chinese Goose

Swan Goose →
Ancestor of the
domestic form

*Pink-footed
Goose*

*Russian
Bean
Goose*
↓

*Johansen's
Bean Goose*

The races of
Bean Goose
all inter-
grade

*Thick-billed
Bean Goose*

*Yellow-billed or
Western Bean Goose*

Middendorf's Bean Goose
↑

*European
White-fronted
Goose*

*Pacific White-fronted
Goose*

Tule Goose
*Greenland
Whitefront*
↓

*European
Whitefront
Adult*

Immature

Black belly
markings of adult
Whitefronts
vary individually
within wide
limits

*Domestic
Embden
Goose*

Drawn to
smaller
scale

*Lesser
White-fronted
Goose*

*Western
Greylag Goose*

Ancestor of
domestic farmyard
geese ; *e.g.*
Toulouse, Embden,
Roman, Sebastopol, etc.

*Eastern
Greylag
Goose*

P.S.

PLATE 4

Bar-headed Goose. *Anser indicus* Latham.

Breeds on lakes of high central Asia from the Tian-Shans to Ladakh and Kokonor. Winters northern India, Assam and northern Burma.

Emperor Goose. *Anser canagicus* Sewastianow.

Breeds on the north-west coast of Alaska from Kotzebue Sound to the Yukon and Kuskokwim Rivers, on St. Lawrence Island and in Siberia from the Anadyr along the Chuckchi Peninsula. Winters in the Aleutian Islands and the Alaska Peninsula, east to Bristol Bay; in Asia, south to the Commander Islands and Kamchatka.

*Lesser Snow Goose and **Blue Goose.** *Anser cærulescens cærulescens* (L.).

Breeds on Baffin and Southampton Islands and Arctic coast of North America from Hudson's Bay westward and in north-eastern Siberia, probably as far west as the Lena. The Blue Goose, formerly regarded as a distinct species, now appears to be a colour phase most numerous at the eastern end of the range, but spreading westwards and becoming more numerous. Nearly all Blue Geese winter on the coast of the Gulf of Mexico, chiefly in Louisiana. Birds of the white phase predominate in California, though some are found on the Gulf coast. In Asia the race occurs south to Japan, but the Siberian population probably winters in America. Individuals of both types have occurred as stragglers in Britain, but some of those recorded may have been escapes.

*Greater Snow Goose. *Anser cærulescens atlanticus* Kennard.

Breeds on the coast of north-west Greenland, Ellesmere Land and the adjacent islands. Migrates by way of Cap Tourmente at mouth of St. Lawrence to winter off Atlantic coast of U.S.A. from Chesapeake Bay to North Carolina. A straggler to Britain, though it is difficult to establish whether records refer to wild birds or to escapes from captivity in this country or elsewhere in Europe.

Ross's Goose. *Anser rossii* Cassin.

Breeds in the Perry River region in the centre of the Arctic coast of Canada. The nest was first found in 1940. Winters in Sacramento and San Joaquin valleys in California. Total population now substantially larger than recorded formerly—at least 70,000 in 1969.

Plate 4

SNOW GEESE, etc.   (ABERRANT GREY GEESE)

The plumage of males and females is the same

Emperor Goose

Ross's Goose

Greater Snow Goose
This race has no blue phase

Lesser Snow Goose
Blue phase Immature

Lesser Snow Goose
Blue phase Adult
White-breasted form

Lesser Snow Goose
White phase Immature

Lesser Snow Goose
Blue phase Typical adult

Lesser Snow Goose
White phase Adult

← These are believed to be two phases of the same sub-species →

Greater Snow Goose

Lesser Snow Goose

Ross's Goose

Bar-headed Goose

P.S.

PLATE 5

*Atlantic Canada Goose. *Branta canadensis canadensis* (L.).
Breeds in south-east Baffin Island, Newfoundland, Labrador east of the Height of Land, and on Magdalen Islands. Winters on Atlantic coast from Nova Scotia south to Florida. Introduced into England first in seventeenth century and now generally regarded as British bird. Also introduced elsewhere in Europe and in New Zealand.

Central or **Todd's Canada Goose.** *Branta canadensis interior* Todd.
Breeds in northern Quebec, Ontario, Manitoba, around southern Hudson Bay and James Bay. Winters from southern Ontario, Wisconsin, Illinois and Chesapeake Bay, along Atlantic coast south to Florida and Louisiana.

Great Basin or **Moffitt's Canada Goose.** *Branta canadensis moffitti* Aldrich.
Breeds from central British Columbia, Alberta and Saskatchewan to north-eastern California, northern Utah, northern Colorado and South Dakota. This race does not move far on migration but has been recorded in winter from southern British Columbia, north-western Wyoming and Arkansas, south to California and the Gulf of Mexico.

Giant Canada Goose. *Branta canadensis maxima* Delacour.
Breeds Minnesota, formerly widespread in great plains of central United States.

Lesser Canada Goose. *Branta canadensis parvipes* (Cassin).
Breeds throughout the interior of northern North America from central Alaska east to Hudson Bay and south to northern British Columbia and Manitoba, where it intergrades with *moffitti* and *interior*. Breeds also on Baffin and Southampton Islands. Migrates mainly west of the Mississippi and winters in southern U.S. from California to Louisiana and south to Mexico.

Taverner's Canada Goose. *Branta canadensis taverneri* Delacour.
Breeds probably in north-west interior from Alaska peninsula to the Perry River, where it intergrades with *parvipes*. Winters from Washington to Texas and Mexico, mainly in California. Also intergrades with *occidentalis*.

Dusky Canada Goose. *Branta canadensis occidentalis* (Baird).
Breeds around Prince William Sound and perhaps farther south along Gulf of Alaska. Usually sedentary, but has been found in Oregon.

Vancouver Canada Goose. *Branta canadensis fulva* Delacour.
Breeds along coast and on islands of British Columbia and southern Alaska. Largely non-migratory but wanderers have been found in northern California in winter.

Aleutian Canada Goose. *Branta canadensis leucopareia* (Brandt).
Now very rare, perhaps breeding only on Buldir Island.

Richardson's Canada Goose. *Branta canadensis hutchinsii* (Richardson).
Breeds on Melville Peninsula, Southampton, Baffin and Ellesmere Islands. Migrates between Mississippi and Rocky Mountains to winter in Texas and Mexico.

Cackling Canada Goose. *Branta canadensis minima* Ridgway.
Breeds along western shores of Alaska. Winters from southern British Columbia to southern California, in large interior valleys.

†Bering Canada Goose. *Branta canadensis asiatica* Aldrich.
Extinct. Bred Bering Island (Commander Islands) and Kurile Islands, until about 1900.

Hawaiian Goose or **Ne-ne.** *Branta sandvicensis* (Vigors).
Breeds on main island of Hawaii. Recently re-introduced on Maui, where has bred. Probably less than 50 left in 1947. More than 1,000 individuals alive at present (1971), about 200 in Britain.

*Barnacle Goose. *Branta leucopsis* (Bechstein)
Three discrete populations: breeds east Greenland, winters west Scotland and Ireland; breeds Spitzbergen, winters Norway and Solway Firth, Scotland; breeds Novaya Zemlya and west Siberian Islands, winters Holland.

*Russian or **Dark-bellied Brent Goose.** *Branta bernicla bernicla* (L.).
Breeds in Arctic Europe and Asia from Kolguev east to Severnaya Zemlya, mainly on Taimyr Peninsula. Winters on coasts of England and north-west Europe.

*Atlantic or **Light-bellied Brent Goose.** *Branta bernicla hrota* (O. F. Müller).
Breeds on coasts and islands of eastern Arctic Canada, northern Greenland, Spitzbergen, Franz Joseph Land. Winters in Ireland, and erratically elsewhere on coasts of north-west Europe, and on Atlantic coast of U.S.A. from New Jersey to North Carolina.

Lawrence's Brent Goose. *Branta bernicla nigricans* (Lawrence).
Breeding area unknown, probably north-east of Hudson's Bay. Winters on coast of New Jersey. Very rare, possibly never existed as a distinct population.

*Pacific Brent Goose or **Black Brant.** *Branta bernicla orientalis* Tougarinov.
Breeds on coasts and islands of western Arctic Canada, northern Alaska and Siberia, west to Taimyr Peninsula. Winters on shores of the Pacific south to Japan and northern China and from Vancouver Island to Lower California, principally in U.S.A. Two records of this race in Britain (1957 and 1958)

*Red-breasted Goose. *Branta ruficollis* (Pallas).
Breeds on the Siberian tundra from the Ob to the Khatanga. Winters in southern part of the Caspian Sea and in the Aral Sea. Scarce in Europe, straggler in Britain.

BLACK GEESE

Plate 5
*Bering
Canada Goose*
Extinct

*Aleutian Canada
Goose*
Apparent tendency to white ring

*Cackling
Goose*

Small
and dark

*Richardson's
Goose*

Small and
pale

*Taverner's Canada
Goose*

*Lesser Canada
Goose*

*Giant
Canada
Goose*

*Dusky Canada
Goose*

*Great Basin
Canada Goose*

*Todd's or →
Central Canada
Goose*

*Atlantic
Canada
Goose*

*Vancouver
Canada
Goose*

*Lawrence's
Brent
Goose*

*Pacific Brent
Goose or Black Brant*

Ring complete
in front

*Russian or
Dark-bellied
Brent
Goose*

*Atlantic or
Light-bellied
Brent*

*Ne-ne or
Hawaiian Goose*

*Barnacle
Goose*

*Red-breasted
Goose*

In all these forms the plumage of both
sexes is the same

P.S.

PLATE 6

Sub-Family ANATINAE

Tribe TADORNINI (Shelducks and Sheldgeese)

†**Crested Shelduck.** *Tadorna cristata* (Kuroda).

Known only from three specimens, two from Korea and one from near Vladivostok. Thought at first to be a hybrid, but figures fairly frequently in ancient Japanese prints, indicating that it is probably a recently extinct species.

***Ruddy Shelduck.** *Tadorna ferruginea* (Pallas).

Breeds in south Spain and from south-east Europe, the Near East, the Caspian Sea, across Asia to Transbaikalia, south to Himalayas and south-western China. Winters in southern half of its breeding range to the Nile Valley; India and southern China. Occasional in Britain.

South African or **Cape Shelduck.** *Tadorna cana* (Gmelin).

Cape Province, Orange Free State and Transvaal.

Australian Shelduck. *Tadorna tadornoides* (Jardine and Selby).

Very numerous in southern South Australia and Victoria and in Tasmania; a straggler further north.

Paradise or **New Zealand Shelduck.** *Tadorna variegata* (Gmelin).

Widespread in North, South and Stewart Islands, New Zealand.

Moluccan or **Black-backed Radjah Shelduck.** *Tadorna radjah radjah* (Lesson).

Moluccas, Ceram, Buru, Waigiu, Salawatti, New Guinea and the Aru Islands.

Australian or **Red-backed Radjah Shelduck** or **Burdekin Duck.** *Tadorna radjah rufitergum* Hartert.

Northern and eastern tropical Australia.

***Common Shelduck.** *Tadorna tadorna* (L.).

Breeds on coasts of western Europe, including the British Isles; locally about the shores of the Mediterranean, Black and Caspian Seas, east on the saline lakes of central Asia to east Siberia, Mongolia and Tibet. Winters from southern part of its breeding range to northern Africa, Arabia, India, south China and Japan.

***Egyptian Goose.** *Alopochen ægyptiacus* (L.).

Africa, south of the Sahara, also the entire Nile Valley; southern Palestine. Occasional records in Europe. Introduced into England, but feral stock remains small.

Orinoco Goose. *Neochen jubatus* (Spix).

Basins of the Orinoco and the Amazon.

44

Plate 6

SHELDUCKS

Common
Shelduck
♀
♂

Crested
Shelduck
♀
♂

Now
extinct

slightly
smaller

Ruddy
Shelduck
♀
♂

Mollucan
Radjah
Shelduck

♂
♂

Cape or
South African
Shelduck
♀
♂

Australian
Radjah
Shelduck

♂ & ♀
the same
in both
races

Australian
Shelduck
or Mountain
Duck
♀
♂

New Zealand
Shelduck or
Paradise Duck
♀
♂

Orinoco
Goose

♂ & ♀
plumage
the
same

Egyptian
Goose

There are two
colour phases, the
second being greyer
on the back than
this one

♂ & ♀
the same

P.S.

PLATE 7

Abyssinian Blue-winged Goose. *Cyanochen cyanopterus* (Rüppell).
Highlands of Abyssinia.

Andean Goose. *Chloëphaga melanoptera* (Eyton).
Western South America from the highlands of Peru and Bolivia to the Straits of Magellan. In winter it descends to the plains at the foot of the Andes in Chile and Argentina.

Ashy-headed Goose. *Chloëphaga poliocephala* Sclater.
Southern Chile and Argentina, Tierra del Fuego; Falkland Islands (rare). Migrates north in winter, but limits of breeding and winter ranges not clearly established.

Ruddy-headed Goose. *Chloëphaga rubidiceps* Sclater.
Falkland Islands and Tierra del Fuego; occasional in Patagonia and central Argentina. Northward movements in winter not yet worked out.

Upland or **Lesser Magellan Goose.** *Chloëphaga picta picta* (Gmelin).
Chile and southern Argentina from the Rio Negro south to Tierra del Fuego. In this form the males may be barred or white-breasted; the barred form predominates near the coast and to the south, the white form inland and to the north.

Falkland Upland or **Greater Magellan Goose.** *Chloëphaga picta leucoptera* (Gmelin).
Falkland Islands. Introduced into South Georgia. Larger than the typical form and males are always white-breasted.

Patagonian or **Lesser Kelp Goose.** *Chloëphaga hybrida hybrida* (Molina).
Coast of Chile from Chiloë, southward to Tierra del Fuego.

Falkland or **Greater Kelp Goose.** *Chloëphaga hybrida malvinarum* Phillips.
Falkland Islands.

Plate 7

SHELDGEESE

All on this page except the Abyssinian are South American

Andean Goose
Male and female plumage the same

Abyssinian Blue-winged Goose

Male and female plumage the same

Falkland Upland or Greater Magellan Goose

♀

♂

Lesser Magellan or Lesser Upland Goose

♂ White form

♀

Males are never barred in this form

♂ Barred form

Ashy-headed Goose

♂ and ♀ the same

♂ and ♀ the same

Ruddy-headed Goose

♀

♂

Falkland Kelp Goose

♀

♂

Patagonian Kelp Goose

Local race with longer bill and legs

P.S.

PLATE 8

Aberrant species with affinities to tribe TADORNINI

Cereopsis or **Cape Barren Goose.** *Cereopsis novæ-hollandiæ* Latham.

Islands off southern coast of Western Australia, South Australia and in Bass Strait. Probably not more than 6,000 individuals at present. This species should probably be placed in a monotypic tribe, Cereopsini.

Flying Steamer Duck. *Tachyeres patachonicus* (King).

Coasts, rivers, and interior lakes of southern South America from Valdivia, Chile on the west and Puerto Deseado, Argentina, on the east, south to Tierra del Fuego; Falkland Islands.

Magellanic Flightless Steamer Duck. *Tachyeres pteneres* (Forster).

The coast of southern South America from Concepcion, Chile, south to Tierra del Fuego, including the Straits of Magellan to the eastern entrance, but not the Atlantic coast north of Cape San Diego.

Falkland Island Flightless Steamer Duck. *Tachyeres brachypterus* (Latham).

Falkland Islands.

Steamer Ducks should probably be placed in a separate tribe, Tachyerini, since their relationship to other ducks remains obscure.

Patagonian Crested Duck. *Lophonetta specularioides specularioides* (King).

From central Chile and west central Argentina south to Tierra del Fuego; Falkland Islands.

Andean Crested Duck. *Lophonetta specularioides alticola* Ménégaux

Highland lakes in the Andes from central Peru, south through Bolivia to the latitude of Santiago, Chile. Occasionally in winter to the central valley of Chile.

Crested Ducks are probably more closely related to the Anatini (Dabbling Ducks) than to the Shelducks.

Plate 8

ABERRANT SPECIES WITH AFFINITIES TO TADORNINI

Larger, with buff chin

Smaller, with white chin and mottled belly

♀

♂

Andean Crested Duck

♀

♂

Patagonian Crested Duck

These Crested Ducks are probably more closely related to the Bronze-winged Ducks than to the Shelducks

Magellanic Steamer is largest, coarsest, palest. Has less red on throat

Falkland Is. Flightless Steamer Duck or Loggerheaded Duck

♀

♂

♀

♂

Magellanic Flightless Steamer Duck

♀

♂

Flying Steamer Duck

♂ and ♀ the same

Flying Steamer is darker and smaller than the other two

Cereopsis or Cape Barren Goose

P.S.

PLATE 9
Tribe ANATINI (Dabbling Ducks)

Marbled Teal. *Marmaronetta (Anas) angustirostris* (Ménétriès).
Resident in Mediterranean Basin from southern Spain to Near East, Persia, Baluchistan and north-western India.

Bronze-winged Duck. *Anas specularis* King.
Slopes of the Andes in Chile and Argentina from the latitude of Concepcion to Tierra del Fuego. North in winter to the vicinity of Valparaiso, Chile.

Salvadori's Duck. *Anas waigiuensis* (Rothschild and Hartert).
Mountains of New Guinea, and possibly the island of Waigiu.

Cape Teal. *Anas capensis* Gmelin.
Africa from Bechuanaland, African lakes, Uganda and southern Abyssinia southward. Apparently not in eastern coastal areas. Recorded from Lake Chad and Senegambia.

Hottentot Teal. *Anas punctata* Burchell.
Africa from Angola, Uganda and Shoa to Cape Province; Madagascar. Recently found Tchad.

Northern Silver or **Versicolor Teal.** *Anas versicolor versicolor* Vieillot.
South America from central Chile, the Bolivian Chaco, Paraguay and southern Brazil, south to central Argentina.

Southern Silver or **Versicolor Teal.** *Anas versicolor fretensis* King.
South America from the latitude of Valdivia, Chile, through southern Chile and Argentina to Tierra del Fuego; Falkland Islands.

Puna Teal. *Anas versicolor puna* Tschudi.
Puna (highland plateau) of the Andes from central Peru, south through Bolivia (Lake Titicaca and Cochabamba) to northern Chile.

Red-billed Pintail. *Anas erythrorhyncha* Gmelin.
South and East Africa from southern Angola, Lakes Tanganyika and Victoria and southern Abyssinia, south to the Cape; Madagascar.

Lesser or **Northern Bahama Pintail.** *Anas bahamensis bahamensis* L.
Bahama Islands, Greater Antilles (Cuba, Haiti, Jamaica, Puerto Rico) northern Lesser Antilles, northern Colombia, the Guianas and northern Brazil, as far as Amazon.

Greater or **Southern Bahama Pintail.** *Anas bahamensis rubrirostris* Vieillot.
Southern Brazil, Paraguay, Uruguay, south to northern and eastern Argentina, and west to eastern Bolivia; central provinces of Chile; recorded on west coast of Peru.

Galapagos Pintail. *Anas bahamensis galapagensis* Ridgway.
Galapagos Islands (Pacific Ocean west of Ecuador).

South Georgian Teal. *Anas georgica georgica* Gmelin.
Island of South Georgia (South Atlantic).

Chilean or **Brown Pintail.** *Anas georgica spinicauda* Vieillot.
South America from southern Colombia and Ecuador, through Bolivia, southern Brazil, Paraguay, Uruguay, Argentina and Chile to Tierra del Fuego; Falkland Islands. Probably does not winter in extreme south of its range.

Niceforo's Pintail. *Anas georgica niceforoi* Wetmore and Borrero.
Eastern Andes of Colombia; also Cali, Valle de Cauca, Colombia. Very rare.

*Northern Pintail. *Anas acuta acuta* L.
Breeds in the northern parts of Europe, Asia and North America, including British Isles. Winters south to North Africa, the Nile Valley, Abyssinia, Persian Gulf, India, Ceylon, Burma, Siam, southern China; from southern British Columbia, Mississippi Valley and Chesapeake Bay to Panama and West Indies; Hawaiian Islands.

Kerguelen or **Eaton's Pintail.** *Anas acuta eatoni* (Sharpe).
Kerguelen Island. Recently introduced into St. Paul and Amsterdam Islands (all in South Indian Ocean).

Crozet Pintail. *Anas acuta drygalskii* Reichenow.
Crozet Islands (South Indian Ocean, 800 miles west of Kerguelen Island.)

Chilean Teal. *Anas flavirostris flavirostris* Vieillot.
South America from central Chile, northwestern Argentina and extreme southern Brazil, south to Tierra del Fuego; Falkland Islands.

Sharp-winged Teal. *Anas flavirostris oxyptera* Meyer.
The Puna zone (highland plateau) of the Andes from northern Peru, south through western Bolivia to northern Chile and northern Argentina.

Andean Teal. *Anas flavirostris andium* (Sclater and Salvin).
High Andes of central and southern Colombia and of Ecuador.

Merida Teal. *Anas flavirostris altipetens* (Conover).
High Andes of western Venezuela and the eastern Andes of Colombia, south to Bogota.

*European Green-winged Teal. *Anas crecca crecca* L.
Breeds in Europe and Asia from Iceland to China, Manchuria and Kurile Islands and Japan. Winters as far south as North Africa, Nile Valley, Somaliland, Persia, India and Ceylon, Assam, southern China and the Philippines.

Aleutian Teal. *Anas crecca nimia* Friedmann.
Aleutian Islands.

*American Green-winged Teal. *Anas crecca carolinensis* Gmelin.
Breeds in northern North America from Alaska to Hudson Bay south to about 40°N. Winters in southern U.S., Mexico, northern Central America and the West Indies. Vagrant to Britain.

50

Bronze-winged Duck

Marbled Teal

Salvadori's Duck

Northern Versicolor Teal ↓

Puna Teal

Cape Teal ↓

Except where shown these are all drakes. The females are duller

These two intergrade ↕

Lesser Bahama Pintail

Southern Versicolor Teal

Hottentot Teal ↓

These two intergrade

Galapagos Pintail

Red-billed Pintail or Red-billed Teal

Greater Bahama Pintail

Niceforo's Pintail

Chilean or Brown Pintail

South Georgian Teal

♂

♀

Pintail

Kerguelen Pintail → ♂

Crozet Is. Pintail ↓ ♂

Merida Teal

Sharp-winged Teal

♀

American ← Green-winged Teal

Aleutian Teal ♂

♂

Andean Teal

European Green-winged Teal ↓

♂

Merida is a lighter version of Andean ♀♀ of these 4 are almost the same as ♂♂

Chilean or Yellow-billed Teal

♀

P.S.

PLATE 10

*Baikal or **Formosa Teal.** *Anas formosa* Georgi.

Breeds in Siberia east from the Yenisei River to the Kolyma delta and Anadyr, south to Lake Baikal, northern Sakhalin and northern Kamchatka. Winters in China and Japan. Recorded from Formosa but derives its name not from the island but from the fact that " formosa " is the Latin for " beautiful.". Two Scotland (1954 and 1958).

Falcated Teal. *Anas falcata* Georgi.

Breeds in northern Asia, south of the Arctic Circle from the Upper Yenesei to Kamchatka, south to Lake Baikal, northern Mongolia, the Amur and Ussuriland. Winters in Japan, Korea, eastern and southern China to Upper Burma.

Madagascar Teal. *Anas bernieri* (Hartlaub).

Western part of Madagascar. Believed to be very rare.

East Indian Grey Teal. *Anas gibberifrons gibberifrons* S. Müller.

East Indies (Java, Celebes, Lesser Sunda Islands, Sabeyer, Sumba, Flores, Timor and Weter).

Rennell Island Grey Teal. *Anas gibberifrons remissa* Ripley.

Rennell Island.

Australian Grey Teal. *Anas gibberifrons gracilis* Buller.

Australia, New Zealand, New Guinea, Aru and Kei Islands and New Caledonia. A recent arrival in New Zealand, where it has spread rapidly.

Andaman Teal. *Anas gibberifrons albogularis* (Hume).

Andaman Islands, Landfall and Great Coco Islands (Indian Ocean). Two races have been described from the islands, but since there is striking individual variation in this species the claim of *A.a. leucopareus* is not substantiated.

Chestnut Teal. *Anas castanea* (Eyton).

Australia (except north coast); abundant in Tasmania and southern Victoria.

Auckland Island Teal. *Anas aucklandica aucklandica* (G. R. Gray).

Auckland Islands (250 miles south of New Zealand). Lately reported to be holding its own satisfactorily, though now very rare on Auckland Island itself.

Campbell Island Teal. *Anas aucklandica nesiotis* (Fleming).

Campbell Island (350 miles south of New Zealand). Only a dozen have ever been seen. Perhaps stragglers from Auckland Islands, rather than a separate race.

New Zealand Brown Teal. *Anas aucklandica chlorotis* G. R. Gray

New Zealand. Rare. Became extinct Chatham Islands about 1915.

DABBLING DUCKS

Baikal or
Formosa Teal

♀ Falcated or
Bronze-capped
Teal
♂

♀

♂

Madagascar
or Bernier's Teal
Erythristic
form of
Grey Teal

← East Indian
Grey Teal High forehead

Rennell Island
Grey Teal
Smallest
of the three

Chestnut
Teal
♀   ♂

Australian
Grey Teal

Andaman ♀
Teal
♂

New Zealand
Brown Duck or
Brown Teal
♀

♂ Dull plumage

Many males
are intermediate
between these
two

♂

Bright
plumage

Island form
of Grey Teal
with variable
amount of
white on
face

Auckland Is.
Teal ♀

♂

Campbell Is.
Teal
♂

Narrower
bill

P.S.

PLATE 11

*Mallard. *Anas platyrhynchos platyrhynchos* L.

Breeds in Europe and Asia from Arctic Circle, south to Mediterranean, Persia, Tibet, central China, Korea and northern Japan; Iceland; the Azores; northern and central North America, west of Hudson's Bay and the Mississippi. Winters from southern half of breeding range to North Africa, Nile Valley, India, Burma, southern China, Japan; southern Mexico and Florida. Successfully introduced New Zealand.

Greenland Mallard. *Anas platyrhynchos conboschas* C. L. Brehm.

Breeds on coasts of Greenland, on the west, north to Upernavik and on the east, north to Angmagssalik.

Florida Duck. *Anas platyrhynchos fulvigula* Ridgway.

Florida, Texas and Louisiana, possibly Alabama. The Mottled Duck *A. fulvigula maculosa* is not now regarded as a separable race.

Mexican Duck. *Anas platyrhynchos diazi* (Ridgway).

Highlands of central Mexico and the upper Rio Grande Valley from El Paso, Texas to Albuquerque, New Mexico.

(Oustalets Duck from the islands of Guam, Saipan and Tinian, 1,200 miles north of New Guinea, was described as a distinct species, or at least race, *A.* (*platyrhynchos*) *oustaleti*, but research by Kuroda has shown this population to result from hybridisation of *A. platyrhynchos* and *A. superciliosa*.)

*North American Black Duck. *Anas rubripes* Brewster.

Breeds in north-eastern North America from the west side of Hudson Bay to Labrador, and south to North Carolina. Winters south to the Gulf coast. Recorded twice in Ireland (1954 and 1961).

Hawaiian Duck. *Anas wyvilliana* Sclater.

Now only on Kaui Island. Fewer than 300 individuals at present.

Laysan Teal. *Anas laysanensis* Rothschild.

Laysan Island (900 miles west of Honolulu). Once very scarce (only 7 individuals left in 1912) but has recently increased substantially, to nearly 700 in 1961.

Indian Spotbill. *Ansa pœcilorhyncha pœcilorhyncha* Forster.

India to western Assam; Ceylon.

Burma Spotbill. *Anas pœcilorhyncha haringtoni* (Oates).

Burma, Shan States, Yunnan.

Chinese Spotbill. *Anas pœcilorhyncha zonorhyncha* Swinhoe.

Breeds in eastern Siberia, Manchuria, Mongolia, northern China, Korea, southern Sakhalin, the Kurile Islands and Japan. Winters south to southern China and Formosa.

New Zealand Grey Duck. *Anas superciliosa superciliosa* Gmelin.

New Zealand and neighbouring islands.

Pelew Island Grey Duck. *Anas superciliosa pelewensis* Hartlaub and Finsch.

Pelew Islands (east of Philippine Islands), northern New Guinea, Solomon Islands, Fiji, Samona, Tonga, Tahiti, New Caledonia, New Hebrides, Bismarck Archipelago.

Australian Black Duck. *Anas superciliosa rogersi* Mathews.

Australia and Tasmania, East Indies, Celebes, Moluccas and New Guinea.

Philippine Duck. *Anas luzonica* Fraser.

Philippine Islands.

Meller's Duck. *Anas melleri* Sclater.

Eastern half of Madagascar; introduced into Mauritius.

African Yellowbill. *Anas undulata undulata* Du Bois.

Africa from Angola, Uganda and Kenya southward.

Abyssinian Yellowbill. *Anas undulata ruppelli* Blyth.

Upper Blue Nile and Abyssinian Lake Region. Probably also Cameroons (one collected).

African Black Duck. *Anas sparsa sparsa* Eyton.

South Africa; northern limits of range not yet known reliably, but as far as Portuguese East Africa and Nyasaland.

Abyssinian Black Duck. *Anas sparsa leucostigma* Rüppell

Abyssinia, Sudan, East Africa across to the Upper Congo, and Tanganyika. Rare in the western part of its range.

Gabon Black Duck. *Anas sparsa maclatchyi* Berlioz.

Western French Equatorial Africa. Probably not a valid race.

54

Plate 11

DABBLING DUCKS (MALLARDS)

Except for the female Mallard all on this page are drakes

Greenland Mallard

Mallard or Wild Duck ♀ ♂

Domestic Duck drawn to smaller scale

North American Black Duck

Mexican Duck

Florida Duck

Black spot

Chinese Spotbill

Indian Spotbill

Burma Spotbill

Females mostly just duller edition of male

Bill deeper yellow

Pelew Island Grey Duck ♂

Smallest

Australian Black Duck

♂ ♂ Largest

Abyssinian Yellowbill ♂

African Yellowbill

♂

Darker

New Zealand Grey Duck Greyer

Gabon Black Duck

← Abyssinian Black Duck

These Black Ducks intergrade

♂

♂ African Black Duck

Philippine Duck

Female similar to male

Laysan Teal

Females also show white round eye

Hawaiian Duck

Female like small female Mallard

Meller's Duck

P.S.

PLATE 12

*Gadwall. *Anas strepera strepera* L.

Europe, Asia and western North America, breeding from Iceland to Kamchatka, British Columbia and Prairie Provinces of Canada, south to England, Holland, Germany, central Russia, Caspian, Siestan, Transbaikalia, California and Colorado. Winters south to northern Africa, Abyssinia, India, Assam, southern China, Lower California, southern Mexico and Florida.

†Coues's Gadwall. *Anas strepera couesi* (Streets).

Washington Is., New York Is. (Fanning Group, 1,000 miles S. of Hawaii). Extinct.

*European Wigeon. *Anas penelope* L.

Europe and Asia, breeding in temperate regions north to the Arctic Circle and beyond, from Iceland and Scotland to Kamchatka. Winters in Britain and south to Nile Valley. Abyssinia, India, southern China and Japan. Regularly in small numbers on the Atlantic coasts of North America, also in British Columbia.

*American Wigeon. *Anas americana* Gmelin.

North America, breeding in the north-west from Alaska to the Prairie Provinces, mainly east of the Rockies and wintering from British Columbia to California and the Gulf Coast, and from Long Island, south to Costa Rica and West Indies. Rare vagrant to Britain.

Chiloe Wigeon. *Anas sibilatrix* Poeppig.

Southern South America from Chile and southern Brazil, south to Tierra del Fuego; Falkland Islands. Breeds in the southern half of its range.

*Prairie Blue-winged Teal. *Anas discors discors* L.

Breeds in central plains of United States north to Great Lakes and Prairie Provinces of Canada. Winters on Gulf coast from Florida to Mexico, in the West Indies, Central America and northern South America to Peru in the west and Cayenne in the north-east. Has probably occurred in Britain, but see under *A.d. orphna.*

*Atlantic Blue-winged Teal. *Anas discors orphna* Stewart and Aldrich.

Breeds in tidal marshes of Atlantic seaboard from New Brunswick, Nova Scotia and Prince Edward Island south to North Carolina. Intergrades with *discors* in Great Lakes region and in central Canada. Part of the population seems to be permanently resident, but many birds migrate to the West Indies and South America. This is probably the the race occurring as a vagrant in Britain. One in 1956 was certainly *orphna*. The validity of this race is contested.

Argentine Cinnamon Teal. *Anas cyanoptera cyanoptera* Vieillot.

Breeds in South America from Southern Peru, Brazil and Uruguay south, and in Falkland Islands.

Andean Cinnamon Teal. *Anas cyanoptera orinomus* (Oberholser).

Puna region (highland plateau) of the Andes in Peru, Bolivia and Chile.

Borrero's Cinnamon Teal. *Anas cyanoptera borreroi* Snyder and Lumsden.

Breeds in highlands of Colombia. Exact limits of range not yet known.

Tropical Cinnamon Teal. *Anas cyanoptera tropica* Snyder and Lumsden.

Lowlands of Colombia.

Northern Cinnamon Teal. *Anas cyanoptera septentrionalium* Snyder and Lumsden.

Breeds in western North America from southern British Columbia to Mexico, east to Kansas and Texas. Winters south to Colombia and Venezuela.

*Garganey. *Anas querquedula* L.

Breeds in southern England, south Sweden, Finland, Russia, east across Asia, south of lat. 60°N. to Kamchatka; southern limits, France, Italy, Black Sea, Turkestan, Manchuria and northern Japan. Winters Mediterranean south to Nigeria, India, Indo-China, Philippines, Celebes, Transvaal, Moluccas and New Guinea.

Argentine Red Shoveler. *Anas platalea* Vieillot.

Southern South America from Peru and Bolivia to southern Brazil and south to Tierra del Fuego and Falkland Islands; migratory in northern and southern parts of its range.

Cape or **South African Shoveler.** *Anas smithi* (Hartert).

South Africa, north to Angola, Bechuanaland and the Transvaal.

Australian Shoveler. *Anas rhynchotis rhynchotis* Latham.

Main strongholds in south-east South Australia and south-west New South Wales.

New Zealand Shoveler. *Anas rhynchotis variegata* (Gould).

New Zealand. Formerly Chatham Islands.

*Common Shoveler. *Anas clypeata* L.

Breeds in Europe, Asia and North America, not north of Arctic Circle nor in eastern Canada. Breeds commonly in Britain. Winters as far south as East Africa, Persian Gulf, Ceylon, Burma, southern China, Japan, Hawaii, Lower California, Mexico, Honduras, Florida.

Plate 12

DABBLING DUCKS

American Wigeon ♂ ♀

Coues's Gadwall Extinct ♀ ♂

Gadwall ♀ ♂

European Wigeon ♀ ♂

Chiloe Wigeon ♀ ♂

Garganey ♀ ♂

Prairie Blue-winged Teal ♀

These probably intergrade ←→

Northern Cinnamon Teal ♀ ♂

Tropical Cinnamon Teal ♀ ♂

← Smallest and spotted

Atlantic Blue-winged Teal ♀ ♂

Argentine Cinnamon Teal ♀ ♂

Andean Cinnamon Teal ♀ ♂

Borrero's Cinnamon Teal ♀

Common Shoveler ♀ ♂

Largest

Cape Shoveler Australian Shoveler ♂

New Zealand Shoveler ♀

Argentine Red Shoveler ♀ ♂

♂

P.S.

PLATE 13

Aberrant species with affinities to the tribe ANATINI

Ringed Teal. *Calonetta leucophrys* Vieillot.

South America from southern Bolivia, Paraguay, south-western and southern Brazil, to north-eastern Argentina and Uruguay. The Ringed Teal is probably more nearly related to the Cairinini (Perching Ducks) than to the Anatini.

Blue or **Mountain Duck.** *Hymenolaimus malacorhynchos* (Gmelin).

Now confined to remote mountain streams of New Zealand. Formerly common, was confined to remote and relatively unmodified localities.

Pink-eared Duck. *Malacorhynchus membranaceus* (Latham).

Inland Australia. Highly nomadic and varies greatly in abundance, depending on rainfall.

†Pink-headed Duck. *Rhodonessa caryophyllacea* (Latham).

North-eastern and eastern India, Nepal and Assam, south to Madras. Was always local and rare, now probably extinct. No reliable reports of wild birds since 1935. Last in captivity died about 1939. Probably a member of the Aythyini (Pochards).

Freckled Duck. *Stictonetta nævosa* (Gould).

The rarest of Australian ducks, perhaps dangerously so. Principal remaining breeding grounds are in South Australia, and are threatened by drainage. This species is possibly a member of the Anserini.

Plate 13 ABERRANT SPECIES WITH AFFINITIES TO DABBLING DUCKS

Ringed Teal

♀

♂

This species seems to be more closely
related to the Perching Ducks than to
the Dabbling Ducks

♀

♂

*Pink-headed
Duck*

Probably now extinct

♀

♂

Male's bill is
only red in
breeding season

Soft flap
at tip of bill

Freckled Duck

Pink-eared Duck

In both these
species ♂ and
♀ are similar

*Blue or
Mountain
Duck*

P.S.

PLATE 14

Tribe **MERGANETTINI** (Torrent Ducks)

Chilean Torrent Duck. *Merganetta armata armata* Gould.

Andes of Chile and adjoining parts of western Argentina, north to Province of Mendoza, south to Tierra del Fuego.

Colombian Torrent Duck. *Merganetta armata colombiana* Des Murs.

Andes of Venezuela, Colombia and northern Ecuador.

Peruvian Torrent Duck. *Merganetta armata leucogenis* (Tschudi).

Andes of central and southern Ecuador and of Peru (except for Tinta, the Cuzcan Andes and Rio Victor—occupied by *M.a. turneri*).

Turner's Torrent Duck. *Merganetta armata turneri* Sclater and Salvin.

Known only from Tinta, the Cuzcan Andes and Rio Victor (Dept. of Arequipa) **Peru.**

Garlepp's or **Bolivian Torrent Duck.** *Merganetta armata garleppi* Berlepsch.

Mountains of Bolivia. Intergrades with *turneri* in the north and *berlepschi* in the south.

Berlepsch's or **Argentine Torrent Duck.** *Merganetta armata berlepschi* Hartert.

Mountains of north-western Argentina (Provinces of Salta and Tucumàn).

Recent work indicates that the last three sub-species are probably no more than variants of *M.a. leucogenis*.

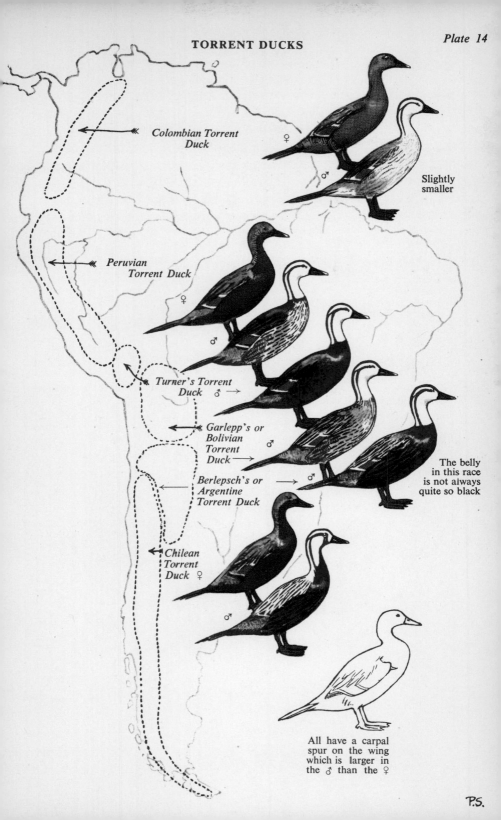

Colombian Torrent Duck ♀

♀

♂

Slightly smaller

Peruvian Torrent Duck ♀

♂

Turner's Torrent Duck ♂ →

Garlepp's or Bolivian Torrent Duck →

♂

Berlepsch's or Argentine Torrent Duck

→ ♂

The belly in this race is not always quite so black

Chilean Torrent Duck ♀

♂

All have a carpal spur on the wing which is larger in the ♂ than the ♀

P.S.

PLATE 15

Tribe SOMATERIINI (Eiders)

*European Eider. *Somateria mollissima mollissima* (L.).

Breeds in Iceland, British Isles, Scandinavia, east to Novaya Zemlya. Mainly resident, but some winter in North Sea and on west coast of France.

Pacific Eider. *Somateria mollissima v-nigra* G. R. Gray.

Breeds on Arctic coasts and islands of north-eastern Asia, Commander and Aleutian Islands and coasts of Alaska and North-West Territories of Canada. Winters chiefly in the Aleutian Islands.

Northern Eider. *Somateria mollissima borealis* (C. L. Brehm).

Breeds on north-eastern coasts of Canada and west Greenland. Winters from the open waters of Greenland, south to Maine.

American Eider. *Somateria mollissima dresseri* Sharpe.

Breeds on both coasts of Hudson's and James Bays and on east coast of Labrador. Winters from Newfoundland to Nantucket.

Faeroe Eider. *Somateria mollissima færoeensis* C. L. Brehm.

Faeroes; resident.

*King Eider. *Somateria spectabilis* (L.).

Breeds on fresh water near the Arctic coasts and on islands of Europe, Asia, and North America. Rare straggler to the British Isles in winter.

Spectacled or **Fischer's Eider.** *Somateria fischeri* (Brandt).

Breeds on the New Siberian Islands and Arctic coast of Siberia from the Yana River to Bering Strait and on the coast of Alaska. Probably winters north of the Aleutian Islands, but range uncertain.

*Steller's Eider. *Polysticta stelleri* (Pallas).

Breeds on the Arctic coast of Siberia from the Taimyr Peninsula to Bering Strait and the coast of Alaska. Winters on open waters of Kamchatka, Commander and Kurile Islands, Aleutian Islands and Kenai Peninsula (Alaska). Rarely recorded in Britain.

The eiders are included in the tribe Mergini by some authorities.

Plate 15

EIDERS

Pacific Eider Largest

Northern Eider Medium sized

First year drakes have only patchy white breast and back

Faeroe Eider Smallest

American or Dresser's Eider Medium

European Eider Large

♀ Pacific

♀ Northern

American

European

Faeroe

Spectacled or Fischer's Eider

King

Spectacled

King Eider

Steller's Eider

P.S.

PLATE 16

Tribe AYTHYINI (Pochards)

*Red-crested Pochard. *Netta rufina* (Pallas).

Eastern Europe and Asia, breeding from southern France, Holland (few), through lower Danube, southern Russia east across Kirghiz Steppes to west Siberia. Winters Mediterranean, India, Burma, Shan States to China. Scarce vagrant in Britain.

Rosybill. *Netta peposaca* (Vieillot).

Central Chile, south to Chiloe Island, east across Argentina to Paraguay, Uruguay and south to northern Patagonia.

South American Pochard. *Netta erythrophthalma erythrophthalma* (Wied).

Western South America from north-western Venezuela to southern Peru.

African Pochard. *Netta erythrophthalma brunnea* (Eyton).

Africa from Angola in the west to Abyssinia and south to Cape Province.

Canvasback. *Aythya valisineria* (Wilson).

North America, breeding in western Prairie Provinces of Canada and west central United States. Wintering from British Columbia, Colorado, southern Illinois and Chesapeake Bay, south to California, central Mexico, the Gulf and Florida.

*European Pochard. *Aythya ferina* (L.).

Breeds in British Isles, southern Scandinavia and central Russia through west Siberia to Lake Baikal, south to Holland, Germany, Balkans, Black Sea, Kirghiz Steppes and Yarkand. Winters in breeding range and south to Nile Valley, India, Burma and south China.

Redhead. *Aythya americana* (Eyton).

Breeds in western North America. Winters in U.S. and south to Lower California and the Valley of Mexico.

Plate 16

POCHARDS

Red-crested
Pochard ♀

♂

Rosybill

♀

♂

South
American
Pochard
Slightly
smaller and
darker

African
Pochard
larger,
paler
♂

Canvasback

♀

♂

Female similar
to female South
American Pochard

To distinguish these
three, note shape of
head, and, in the
males, the colour of
the back and of the
eye

♀

♂

Redhead ♀

Round
head

♂

European Pochard

♂ & ♀.

P.S.

PLATE 17

Madagascar White-eye. *Aythya innotata* (Salvadori).
Northern and eastern Madagascar.

*Common White-eye or **Ferruginous Duck.** *Aythya nyroca* (Güldenstädt).
Breeds in southern Europe, Balkans, Poland and west Siberia to the Ob Valley, south to northern Africa, Persia, Turkestan, Kashmir, the Pamirs and southern Tibet. Winters in the Mediterranean, Nile Valley, Persian Gulf, India and Burma. Rare vagrant in Britain.

Baer's Pochard. *Aythya baeri* (Radde).
Breeds from Transbaikalia to the lower Ussuri and the Amur. Winters in China, Korea, Japan, upper Assam and Burma.

Australian White-eye or **Hardhead.** *Aythya australis australis* (Eyton).
Australia, New Guinea, New Caledonia, casual in some East Indies. Formerly New Zealand.

Banks Island White-eye. *Aythya australis extima* Mayr.
Banks and Gaua Islands (north of New Hebrides).

New Zealand Scaup or **Black Teal.** *Aythya novæ-seelandiæ* (Gmelin).
New Zealand, Auckland Islands, Chatham Islands.

*Ring-necked Duck. *Aythya collaris* (Donovan).
Breeds in central and north-western North America. Winters in southern U.S., south to Guatemala and West Indies. Accidental in Britain (five records, 1801, 1955, 1959, 1962, 1963).

*Tufted Duck. *Aythya fuligula* (L.).
Breeds in Europe and Asia from Iceland and British Isles to the Commander Islands (Pacific), south to central Europe, Balkans, Kirghiz Steppes, Lake Baikal, the Amur and Sakhalin. Winters in southern half of breeding range and south to Nile Valley, Persian Gulf, India, south China and Philippines.

Lesser Scaup. *Aythya affinis* (Eyton).
Breeds in north-central and north-western Canada and U.S. Winters in southern U.S., south to Panama and West Indies.

*European Scaup. *Aythya marila marila* (L.).
Breeds in northern Europe and Asia, east to the Lena. Has bred Scotland. Winters on coasts of western Europe (including Britain), eastern Mediterranean, Black Sea, Persian Gulf, north-western India.

Pacific Greater Scaup. *Aythya marila mariloides* (Vigors).
Breeds in North America from Hudson's Bay to the Aleutians, Bering Island, Kamchatka and probably elsewhere on the eastern Asiatic mainland. Winters on Pacific and Atlantic coasts of North America, south to Lower California and the West Indies, also China, Korea and Japan.

Baer's Pochard

Common
White-eye
or Ferruginous
Duck

Banks Island
White-eye
Smaller

Madagascar
White-eye

Some females
have white under
tail, especially
in autumn

Australian
White-eye

Ring-neck
or Ring-bill

Tufted
Duck

Lesser
Scaup
or Little Blue-bill

New Zealand
Scaup
or " Black Teal "

Female in
summer

European Scaup

Pacific Greater Scaup
Blue-bill or Broad-bill

Slightly smaller and darker on back

P.S.

PLATE 18

Tribe CAIRININI (Wood Ducks or Perching Ducks and Geese)

Lesser Brazilian Teal. *Amazonetta brasiliensis brasiliensis* (Gmelin).

Eastern South America from the Orinoco, western Brazil, eastern Bolivia, Paraguay, Uruguay and northern Argentina. There is a light and a dark colour phase of this race.

Greater Brazilian or Schuyl's Teal. *Amazonetta brasiliensis ipecutiri* Vieillot.

Argentina, south of Buenos Aires. The ranges of the races of *A. brasiliensis* are probably complicated by some migration. It is possible that more than two races exist.

Australian Wood Duck or **Maned Goose.** *Chenonetta jubata* (Latham).

Inland Australia.

*Mandarin Duck. *Aix galericulata* (L.).

Eastern Asia from the Amur and Ussuri, south through Korea, eastern China, Japan to Formosa. Females from Korea are darker than those from elsewhere and have pink bills, and this population may constitute a distinct race. Introduced and now well established in England.

North American Wood Duck. *Aix sponsa* (L.).

Eastern half of the United States and southern Canada. Wintering in southern and south-eastern States. Also in the west from British Columbia to California (an entirely separate population).

African Pygmy Goose. *Nettapus auritus* (Boddaert).

Africa from a line between Gambia and Kenya, south to the Cape along the coastal belt only, and Madagascar.

Green Pygmy Goose. *Nettapus pulchellus* Gould.

Ceram, Buru, southern New Guinea, northern Australia.

Indian Pygmy Goose or **Cotton Teal.** *Nettapus coromandelianus coromandelianus* (Gmelin).

India, Ceylon, Burma, east to southern China, south to Malaya and north-western East Indies.

Australian Pygmy Goose, *Nettapus coromandelianus albipennis* Gould.

North-eastern Australia, nowhere abundant.

Plate 18

PERCHING DUCKS

Lesser Brazilian Teal

Dark Phase

Light Phase

♀ ♂ ♀ ♂

How to distinguish the females and eclipse plumage males of ←—Mandarin

from *Carolina* ↘

Although apparently closely related no hybrid between Mandarin and Carolina has been recorded, probably due to chromosome differences

These two races intergrade. Other distinguishable races may exist

Greater Brazilian or Schuyl's Teal

♀ ♂

Mandarin Duck
♂ with crest depressed

♀

♂ with crest spread

Carolina or Wood Duck

Australian Wood Duck or Maned Goose

♀ ♂

Indian Pygmy Goose or Cotton Teal

♀ ♂

Slightly larger than Indian race

♀ ♂

Australian Pygmy Goose

African Pygmy Goose

♀ ♂

♀

♂

Green Pygmy Goose

P.S.

PLATE 19

Comb Duck. *Sarkidiornis melanotos melanotos* (Pennant).

Africa from Gambia and the Sudan, south to the Cape and Madagascar; India, Ceylon, Burma and south-eastern China.

South American Comb Duck. *Sarkidiornis melanotos carunculatus* (Lichtenstein).

Eastern tropical South America from Venezuela, south to southern Brazil, Paraguay and northern Argentina.

Western Hartlaub's Duck. *Pteronetta hartlaubi hartlaubi* (Cassin).

West and central Africa (Liberia eastwards; limits of range not known). Probably intergrades with *albifrons*.

Eastern Hartlaub's Duck. *Pteronetta hartlaubi albifrons* (Neumann).

African Lake Region and Congo westwards at least to Ituri River. Probably intergrades westward with *hartlaubi*.

White-winged Wood Duck. *Cairina scutulata* (S. Müller).

Assam, south through Malaya to Sumatra and Java. Sumatran and perhaps Javan birds may belong to a separable race.

Muscovy Duck. *Cairina moschata* (L.).

Mexico, south through central America and South America to Peru on the west and to Uruguay in the east. The ancestor of the farmyard Muscovy Duck.

Spur-winged Goose. *Plectropterus gambensis gambensis* (L.).

Africa from Gambia to upper Nile, south to the Zambesi.

Black Spur-winged Goose. *Plectropterus gambensis niger* P. L. Sclater.

Africa, south of the Zambesi.

Plate 19

PERCHING DUCKS
AND GEESE

South American
Comb Duck

♀ ♂

Comb Duck
or Knob-bill

♀ ♂

Western
Hartlaub's
Duck

♀ ♂

Eastern
Hartlaub's
Duck

♂

White-winged
Wood Duck

♂ and ♀ the same

Spur-winged
Goose

♀ ♂

In both
races there is
a carpal spur,
larger in the
male. It is normally
hidden.

Domestic Muscovy, which
may be glossy green, grey
or white, or a mixture

♀ ♂

♀ ♂

Wild Muscovy
Duck

The species from which the
farmyard Muscovy was
originally domesticated

Black Spur-winged
Goose

The two races of Spurwings
intergrade

P.S.

PLATE 20

Tribe MERGINI (Scoters, Goldeneyes, Mergansers)

†Labrador Duck. *Camptorhynchus labradorius* (Gmelin).

Now extinct. Formerly bred in Labrador. Wintered south, probably to Chesapeake Bay, but chiefly off Long Island. Last one shot in 1875.

*Common or **Black Scoter.** *Melanitta nigra nigra* (L.).

Breeds in Iceland, Ireland, Scotland, northern Europe and Asia from Norway, east to the Taimyr Peninsula. Winters chiefly on coasts of western Europe (including Britain), Mediterranean, Black and Caspian Seas.

American Black Scoter. *Melanitta nigra americana* (Swainson).

Breeds in north-eastern Asia, Aleutian Islands, western Alaska, sporadically across northern North America to Newfoundland. Winters south to China and Japan, California, North Carolina, and on Great Lakes.

*Surf Scoter. *Melanitta perspicillata* (L.).

Breeds in northern North America, west of Hudson's Bay in Labrador and possibly in north-eastern Siberia. Winters from Alaska to California, on the Great Lakes, and from Nova Scotia to South Carolina. Occasional in Britain.

*Velvet or **European White-winged Scoter.** *Melanitta fusca fusca* (L.).

Breeds from Scandinavia and the Baltic, east to Yenisei. Winters on the coasts of western Europe (including Britain), the Mediterranean, Black and Caspian Seas.

Asiatic White-winged Scoter. *Melanitta fusca stejnegeri* (Ridgway).

Breeds in eastern Asia from the Altai to Anadyr, Kamchatka and the Commander Islands. Winters on Pacific coast south to China and Japan.

Pacific White-winged Scoter. *Melanitta fusca dixoni* (Brooks).

Breeds in western Alaska. Winters on Pacific coast of North America, south to California. There is some considerable doubt whether this race can justifiably be separated from *deglandi*.

American White-winged Scoter. *Melanitta fusca deglandi* (Bonaparte).

Breeds in north-western Canada from the Mackenzie to James Bay and south to North Dakota. Winters on the Great Lakes and Atlantic coast, south to North Carolina.

Plate 20

SCOTERS

Bills of drake Scoters

Nail of bill more curved in both sexes

American Black Scoter

Common or Black Scoter

Labrador Duck Extinct

Surf Scoter

Black

American Black

Surf

Asiatic White-winged

Velvet

American White-winged

As above but shorter

Pacific White-winged

The females of all four races of Velvet Scoter are almost exactly alike

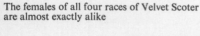

Pacific White-winged Scoter

American White-winged Scoter

♂ and ♀

Velvet Scoter

Asiatic White-winged Scoter

P.S.

PLATE 21

*Atlantic Harlequin Duck. *Histrionicus histrionicus histrionicus* (L.).

Iceland, Greenland, northern Labrador. Mainly resident, breeding on rivers and wintering on sea coasts; some south to Long Island in winter. Rare straggler to Britain.

Pacific or **Western Harlequin Duck.** *Histrionicus histrionicus pacificus* W. S. Brooks.

Breeds in eastern Siberia from the Lena and Lake Baikal to Anadyr, Kamchatka, Sakhalin and the Kurile Islands. In North America from southern Alaska, south in the mountains to central California and Colorado. Winters on coasts south to Japan and California. This race is probably invalid.

*Long-tailed Duck or **Old Squaw.** *Clangula hyemalis* (L.).

Breeds on Arctic coasts of Europe, Asia and North America. Winters south to Britain, France, Holland, Black Sea, Caspian Sea, Japan, California, the Great Lakes, North Carolina; southern Greenland.

Barrow's Goldeneye. *Bucephala islandica* (Gmelin).

Breeds in Iceland, south-western Greenland, Labrador and in the mountains of north-western North America from south-central Alaska to south-western Colorado. The birds of Iceland and Greenland are resident, repairing to the coast in winter. Those in America winter south to Long Island on the Atlantic coast and San Francisco on the Pacific. Females with largely yellow bills occur often in the Rocky Mountain population but apparently not in the other parts of the breeding range and the two groups may form valid races.

*European Goldeneye. *Bucephala clangula clangula* (L.).

Breeds from northern Scandinavia east across Eurpoe and Asia, north to the limit of trees, south to Germany, Balkans, central Russia and Siberia to Kamchatka and Sakhalin. Winters from British Isles, Mediterranean, northern India, to southern China and Japan.

American Goldeneye. *Bucephala clangula americana* (Bonaparte).

Breeds in North America in heavy timber from Alaska and British Columbia to Newfoundland. Winters on Pacific coast south to California and on Atlantic to South Carolina. Also on open lakes and rivers in central United States.

*Bufflehead. *Bucephala albeola* (L.).

Breeds from central Alaska to Hudson's Bay, south to British Columbia, Alberta and Manitoba. Winters mainly in the United States; also Aleutian and Commander Islands. Rare vagrant to Britain.

74

Plate 21

HARLEQUINS, LONGTAIL and GOLDENEYES

Darker chestnut streak

♂

Atlantic Harlequin

White goes farther back

Paler → streak

Heavier bill

♂ *Pacific Harlequin*

Slightly larger bird

The Longtail has two strikingly different plumages—summer and winter (and an eclipse in the drake in autumn)

♀ Showing → wholly yellow bill

♀

Barrow's Goldeneye

♀

♂

Bufflehead

♀ ♂ ♀ *Atlantic Harlequin Duck* ♂

Pacific or Western Harlequin

♀ ♂ *Long-tailed Duck or Old Squaw*

Summer

♀ ♂ Winter

♀ ♂ *American Goldeneye* Larger

♀ ♂ *European Goldeneye* Smaller

P.S.

PLATE 22

*Smew. *Mergus albellus* L.

Breeds in Europe and Asia from Scandinavia to Siberia and south to the Volga, Turkestan and the Amur. Winters on coasts and lakes from Britain (regular on reservoirs near London), the Mediterranean, Persia, northern India to China and Japan.

*Hooded Merganser. *Mergus cucullatus* L.

North America, breeding from south central Canada to southern U.S. and wintering chiefly in the Pacific States, Great Lakes, the Gulf States and Atlantic States south of New York. Rare vagrant to Britain.

Brazilian Merganser. *Mergus octosetaceus* Vieillot.

Southern Brazil, eastern Paraguay and north-eastern Argentina.

†Auckland Islands Merganser. *Mergus australis* Hombron & Jacquinot.

Found on Auckland Islands (250 miles south of New Zealand) from 1840 to 1902, but not since. Sub-fossil bones also found on east coast of South Island, New Zealand.

*Red-breasted Merganser. *Mergus serrator serrator* L.

Breeds in suitable places throughout northern Europe, Asia, and North America (including British Isles), south in winter to the Mediterranean, Persian Gulf, China, Formosa, Gulf of Mexico and Florida.

Greenland Merganser. *Mergus serrator schioleri* Salomonsen.

Resident in Greenland.

Chinese or **Scaly-sided Merganser.** *Mergus squamatus* Gould.

Recorded in summer from Copper Island on the lower Amur River. Winters in China from western Szechuan to central Fukien and south to western Yunnan.

*Goosander. *Mergus merganser merganser* L.

Breeds in Europe and Asia from Iceland, British Isles, Switzerland, the Balkans, to Kamchatka, the Kurile and Commander Islands. South in winter to Mediterranean and China.

Asiatic Goosander. *Mergus merganser orientalis* Gould.

Afghanistan, Turkestan, Altai, Tibet. Winters northern India, northern Burma and China (Szechuan) and farther east, where it occurs with the typical race.

American Merganser. *Mergus merganser americanus* Cassin.

North America, breeding south of a line from south-eastern Alaska to James Bay; and wintering south to the Gulf of Mexico.

Plate 22

MERGANSERS or SAWBILLS

Hooded
Merganser

♀

♂

♀

♂

Smew

Greenland
Merganser
Thicker Bill

♀

♂

♀

♂

Red-breasted
Merganser

Goosander

Red-breasted
Merganser

American
Merganser

♀

♂

Goosander

♀

Nail
hooked

♂

Asiatic
Goosander
Smaller

♀

♂

Chinese Merganser

Brazilian
Merganser
♂ and ♀
similar

♂. ♀ had
single white
wing bar

Auckland
Islands Merganser
Extinct

P.S.

PLATE 23

Tribe OXYURINI (Stiff-tails)

Masked Duck. *Oxyura dominica* (L.).
Greater Antilles (Cuba, Haiti, Jamaica, Puerto Rico) and South America to central Chile and north-eastern Argentina.

White-headed Stiff-tail. *Oxyura leucocephala* (Scopoli).
Mediterranean, Black and Caspian Seas, Turkestan, south in winter to Egypt, Palestine, Mesopotamia and northern India.

North American Ruddy Duck. *Oxyura jamaicensis jamaicensis* (Gmelin).
Breeds in north-west central North America and winters south to California, Mexico, Florida and the Carolinas; also resident in West Indies. West Indian birds have been separated from N. American, the latter being named *O.j. rubida*, but the distinction is doubtful. Birds escaped from captivity are now breeding on at least three reservoirs in England.

Colombian Ruddy Duck. *Oxyura jamaicensis andina* Lehmann.
Andean lakes of central and eastern Colombia. This race forms the link between *O.j. jamaicensis* and *O.j. ferruginea* and may intergrade in both directions.

Peruvian Ruddy Duck. *Oxyura jamaicensis ferruginea* (Eyton).
Andean lakes of Peru and Bolivia. Birds from Ecuador have been separated as *O.f. æquatorialis* but in view of the apparently exceptional individual variation it is doubtful if this race can be accepted.

Argentine Ruddy Duck. *Oxyura vittata* (R. A. Philippi).
Southern South America from northern Chile and southern Brazil to Tierra del Fuego. This species and *O.j. ferruginea* have been found breeding on the Lago Peñuelas, near Valparaiso, which indicates that they must be regarded as specifically distinct.

Australian Blue-billed Duck. *Oxyura australis* (Gould).
In dense swamps in southern Australia.

African Maccoa Duck. *Oxyura maccoa* (Eyton).
Eastern Africa from southern Abyssinia to the Cape.

Musk Duck. *Biziura lobata* (Shaw).
Southern Australia and Tasmania; in deep, permanent swamps.

Africa White-backed Duck. *Thalassornis leuconotus leuconotus* Eyton.
Africa from eastern Cameroon and southern Abyssinia, south to the Cape.

Madagascar White-backed Duck. *Thalassornis leuconotus insularis* Richmond.
Madagascar.

Black-headed Duck. *Heteronetta atricapilla* (Merrem).
Central Chile, east to Paraguay and southern Brazil, south in Argentina at least to the latitude of Buenos Aires.

Recent behavioural and anatomical work suggests that the genus *Thalassornis* may be more closely related to the tribe *Dendrocygnini* than to the *Oxyurini.*

Plate 23

STIFF-TAILS

Two normal swimming positions

♂ displaying

Tail spread

White-headed Stiff-tail

♀

♂

North American Ruddy Duck

Winter ♂

♀

Summer ♂ →

Peruvian Ruddy Duck

broad bill

♀

Masked Duck

♀

♂

♂

Colombian Ruddy Duck

♀

♂

These three races intergrade, the white cheeks (not always present in *andina*) are progressively lost

Maccoa Duck

♀

♂

♀

♂

narrow bill

♀

♂

Australian Blue-billed Duck

Argentine Ruddy Duck

♀

♂

Madagascar White-backed Duck

Normal swimming position

African White-backed Duck ♂ and ♀ the same

Smaller and brighter ♂ and ♀ the same

Black-headed Duck

♀

♂

Parasitic, laying in other bird's nests

♂ and ♀

♀

♂

Musk Duck

P.S

INDEX OF SCIENTIFIC NAMES

Figures opposite names refer to plate numbers. Names of genera are shown in capitals, of species and subspecies in roman type. Where a species includes several subspecies the subspecific name only is cited with that of the genus: e.g., *Dendrocygna arcuata arcuata* is listed as 'arcuata, Dendrocygna' while *Dendrocygna arcuata australis* appears as 'australis, Dendrocygna'. The names of genera and species shown in parenthesis are synonyms no longer in use. Only names which have been widely used, but are now discarded, are included in the synonymy.

	Plate			Plate
acuta, Anas..	9	(ARCTONETTA) Somateria		
aegyptiacus, Alopochen	6	fischeri		15
(aequatorialis) Oxyura		arcuata, Dendrocygna		1
ferruginea	23	armata, Merganetta		14
affinis, Aythya	17	(arvensis) Anser fabalis		3
AIX	18	(ASARCORNIS) Cairina		
albellus, Mergus	22	scutulata ..		19
albeola, Bucephala	21	asiatica, Branta		5
albifrons, Anser	3	atlanticus, Anser		4
albifrons, Pteronetta	19	atratus, Cygnus		2
albipennis, Nettapus	18	atricapilla, Heteronetta		23
albogularis, Anas ..	10	aucklandica, Anas..		10
ALOPOCHEN ..	6	auritus, Nettapus ..		18
alticola, Lophonetta	8	australis, Aythya		17
altipetens, Anas	9	australis, Dendrocygna		1
AMAZONETTA	18	australis, Mergus ..		22
americana, Anas	12	australis, Oxyura		23
americana, Aythya	16	autumnalis, Dendrocygna		1
americana, Bucephala	21	AYTHYA		16, 17
americana, Melanitta	20			
americanus, Mergus	22			
ANAS..	9 to 12	baeri, Aythya		17
andina, Oxyura	23	bahamensis, Anas ..		9
andium, Anas	9	berlepschi, Merganetta		14
angustirostris, Marmaronetta	9	bernicla, Branta		5
ANSER	3, 4	bernieri, Anas		10
anser, Anser	3	bewickii, Cygnus		2
ANSERANAS ..	1	bicolor, Dendrocygna		1
arborea, Dendrocygna	1	BIZIURA		23

Plate

borealis, Somateria .. 15
borreroi, Anas 12
brachypterus, Tachyeres .. 8
brachyrhynchus, Anser .. 3
BRANTA 5
brasiliensis, Amazonetta .. 18
brunnea, Netta 16
buccinator, Cygnus .. 2
BUCEPHALA 21

CAIRINA 19
CALONETTA 13
CAMPTORHYNCHUS 20
cana, Tadorna 6
canadensis, Branta.. .. 5
canagicus, Anser 4
capensis, Anas 9
carolinensis, Anas 9
carunculatus, Sarkidiornis 19
caryophyllacea, Rhodonessa 13
(CASARCA) part of TADORNA 6
castanea, Anas 10
CEREOPSIS 8
(CHAULELASMUS) Anas
 strepera 12
(CHEN) part of ANSER .. 4
(CHENISCUS) part of
 NETTAPUS.. 18
CHENONETTA 18
(CHENOPIS) Cygnus atratus 2
chlorotis, Anas 10
CHLOEPHAGA 7
CLANGULA 21
clangula, Bucephala .. 21
clypeata, Anas 12
cœrulescens, Anser .. 4
collaris, Aythya 17
colombiana, Merganetta .. 14
colombianus, Cygnus .. 2
conboschas, Anas 11
coromandelianus, Nettapus 18
COSCOROBA 2

Plate

couesi, Anas 12
crecca, Anas 9
cristata, Tadorna 6
cucullatus, Mergus .. 22
CYANOCHEN 7
cyanoptera, Anas 12
cyanopterus, Cyanochen .. 7
cygnoides, Anser 3
(CYGNOPSIS) Anser
 cygnoides 3
CYGNUS 2
cygnus, Cygnus 2

(DAFILA) part of ANAS .. 9
deglandi, Melanitta .. 20
DENDROCYGNA 1
(DENDRONESSA) Aix
 galericulata 18
diazi, Anas 12
discolor, Dendrocygna .. 1
discors, Anas 12
(dispar) Chloephaga p. picta 7
dixoni, Melanitta 20
dominica, Oxyura 23
dresseri, Somateria .. 15
drygalskii, Anas 9

eatoni, Anas 9
(ERISMATURA) OXYURA .. 23
erythrophthalma, Netta .. 16
erythropus, Anser 3
erythrorhyncha, Anas .. 9
(EULABEIA) Anser indicus .. 4
(EUNETTA) Anas falcata .. 10
extima, Aythya 17
eytoni, Dendrocygna .. 1

fabalis, Anser 3
faerœensis, Somateria .. 15
falcata, Anas 10

82

Plate   *Plate*

ferina, Aythya 16
ferrginuea, Oxyura .. 23
ferruginea, Tadorna .. 6
fischeri, Somateria .. 15
flavirostris, Anas 9
flavirostris, Anser 3
formosa, Anas 10
(frænata) Merganetta
   armata armata 14
fretensis, Anas 9
frontalis, Anser 3
(FULIGULA) part of AYTHYA 17
fuligula, Aythya 17
fulva, Branta 5
(fulva) Dendrocygna bicolor 1
fulvigula, Anas 11
fusca, Melanitta 20

galapagensis, Anas .. 9
galericulata, Aix 18
gambelli, Anser 3
gambensis, Plectropterus .. 19
garleppi, Merganetta .. 14
georgica, Anas 9
gibberifrons, Anas .. 10
(GLAUCIONETTA) BUCEPHALA 21
gracilis, Anas 10
guttata, Dendrocygna .. 1

haringtoni, Anas 11
hartlaubi, Pteronetta .. 19
HETERONETTA 23
HISTRIONICUS 21
histrionicus, Histrionicus .. 21
hrota, Branta 5
hutchinsii, Branta 5
hybrida, Chloephaga .. 7
hyemalis, Clangula .. 21
HYMENOLAIMUS 13
(hyperborea) Anser
   cœrulescens 4

indicus, Anser 4
innotata, Aythya 17
insularis, Thalassornis .. 23
interior, Branta 5
ipecutiri, Amazonetta .. 18
islandica, Bucephala .. 21
(islandicus) Cygnus cygnus 2

jamaicensis, Oxyura .. 23
jankowskii, Cygnus .. 2
javanica, Dendrocygna .. 1
johanseni, Anser 3
jubata, Chenonetta .. 18
jubatus, Neochen 6

labradorius,
   Camptorhynchus .. 20
laysanensis, Anas 11
leucocephala, Oxyura .. 23
leucogenis, Merganetta .. 14
leuconotus, Thalassornis .. 23
leucopareia, Branta .. 5
leucophrys, Anas 13
leucopsis, Branta 5
leucoptera, Chloephaga .. 7
leucostigma, Anas 11
lobata, Biziura 23
(LOPHODYTES) Mergus
   cucullatus 22
LOPHONETTA 8
luzonica, Anas 11

maccoa, Oxyura 23
maclatchyi, Anas 11
(maculosa) Anas
   platyrhynchos fulvigula.. 11
(major) Mergus serrator
   schioleri 22
malacorhynchos,
   Hymenolaimus 13

	Plate		Plate
MALACORHYNCHUS	13	(NETTION) part of ANAS	9, 10, 13
malvinarum, Chloephaga ..	7	and Amazonetta	
(MARECA) part of ANAS ..	12	brasiliensis	18
marila, Aythya	17	niceforoi, Anas	9
mariloides, Aythya ..	17	niger, Plectropterus ..	19
MARMARONETTA	9	nigra, Melanitta	20
(mathewsi) Anas gibberi-		nigricans, Branta	5
frons gracilis	10	nimia, Anas	9
maxima, Branta	5	(nivalis) Anser cœrulescens	4
MELANITTA	20	(NOMONYX) Oxyura	
melanocoryphus, Cygnus ..	2	dominica	23
melanoptera, Chloephaga..	7	novæ-hollandiæ, Cereopsis	8
melanotos, Sarkidiornis ..	19	novæ-seelandiæ, Aythya ..	17
melleri, Anas	11	(novimexicana) Anas	
membranaceus, Malaco-		platyrhynchos diazi ..	11
rhynchus	13	(NYROCA) AYTHYA ..	16, 17
MERGANETTA	14	nyroca, Aythya	17
merganser, Mergus ..	22		
(MERGELLUS) Mergus			
albellus	22	occidentalis, Branta ..	5
MERGUS	22	octosetaceus, Mergus ..	22
(METOPIANA) Netta		(OIDEMIA) Melanitta nigra..	20
peposaca	16	olor, Cygnus	2
middendorfi, Anser ..	3	orientalis, Branta	5
minima, Branta	5	orientalis, Mergus	22
moffitti, Branta	5	orinomus, Anas	12
mollissima, Somateria ..	15	orphna, Anas	12
moschata, Cairina	19	(oustaleti) Anas platyrhyn-	
		chos x A. superciliosa ..	11
		oxyptera, Anas	9
		OXYURA	23
nævosa, Stictonetta ..	13		
(nearctica) Aythya marila			
mariloides	17	pacificus, Histrionicus ..	21
(neglectus) Anser f. fabalis	3	parvipes, Branta	5
NEOCHEN	6	patachonicus, Tachyeres ..	8
nesiotis, Anas	10	pelewensis, Anas	11
(NESOCHEN) Branta		penelope, Anas	12
sandvicensis	5	peposaca, Netta	16
(NESONETTA) Anas		(percna) Anas superciliosa	
aucklandica	10	rogersi	11
NETTA	16	perspicillata, Melanitta ..	20
NETTAPUS	18	(PHILACTE) Anser canagicus	4

84

	Plate		Plate
picta, Chloephaga	7	SARKIDIORNIS	19
platalea, Anas	12	schioleri, Mergus	22
platyrhynchos, Anas ..	11	scutulata, Cairina	19
PLECTROPTERUS	19	(sedentaria) Somateria	
poecilorhyncha, Anas ..	11	mollissima dresseri ..	15
poliocephala, Chloephaga	7	semipalmata, Anseranas ..	1
POLYSTICTA	15	septentrionalium, Anas ..	12
(PSEUDOTADORNA) Tadorna		serrator, Mergus	22
cristata	6	serrirostris, Anser ..	3
pteneres, Tachyeres ..	8	sibilatrix, Anas	12
PTERONETTA..	19	(sibiricus) Anser fabalis	
pulchellus, Nettapus ..	18	middendorfi	3
puna, Anas	9	smithi, Anas	12
(PUNANETTA) Anas		SOMATERIA	15
versicolor	9	sparsa, Anas	11
punctata, Anas	9	(SPATULA) part of ANAS ..	12
pygmæa, Dendrocygna ..	1	spectabilis, Somateria ..	15
		specularioides, Lophonetta	8
		specularis, Anas	9
(QUERQUEDULA) part of ANAS	12	spinicauda, Anas	9
querquedula, Anas ..	12	sponsa, Aix	18
		squamatus, Mergus ..	22
		stejnegeri, Melanitta ..	20
radjah, Tadorna	6	stelleri, Polysticta	15
remissa, Anas	10	STICTONETTA	13
RHODONESSA	13	strepera, Anas	12
rhynchotis, Anas	12	superciliosa, Anas	11
rogersi, Anas	11	(sylvestris) Anser a. anser..	3
rossicus, Anser	3	(sylvicola), Sarkidiornis	
rossii, Anser	4	melanotus carunculatus	19
rubidiceps, Chloephaga ..	7		
rubripes, Anas	11		
rubrirostris, Anas	9		
rubrirostris, Anser ..	3	TACHYERES	8
ruficollis, Branta	5	TADORNA	6
rufina, Netta	16	tadorna, Tadorna	6
rufitergum, Tadorna ..	6	tadornoides, Tadorna ..	6
ruppelli, Anas	11	taverneri, Branta	5
		THALASSORNIS	23
		(torquatum) Anas	
(SALVADORINA) Anas		leucophrys	13
waigiuensis	9	(tristis) Anas rubripes ..	11
sandvicensis, Branta ..	5	tropica, Anas	12

	Plate			Plate
turneri, Merganetta	.. 14	(vittata) Amazonetta		
(tzitzihoa) Anas a. acuta	.. 9	brasiliensis ipecutiri	..	18
		vittata, Oxyura ..	..	23
		v-nigra, Somateria	..	15
undulata, Anas ..	.. 11			
		waigiuensis, Anas ..	..	9
vallisneria, Aythya..	.. 16	wyvilliana, Anas ..	..	11
variegata, Anas ..	.. 12			
variegata, Tadorna	.. 6			
versicolor, Anas ..	.. 9			
viduata, Dendrocygna	.. 1	zonorhyncha, Anas	..	11

INDEX OF ENGLISH NAMES

The application of English names to birds is not governed by formal procedure such as governs the scientific terminology. This index is correspondingly unsystematic. It aims at enabling the reader to find the illustrations of every species, and so it includes a number of names in local or general use even though alternative names have been employed in the text. Such additional names are shown in italic type, followed immediately by the preferred name, in roman type.

Although it seemed desirable to provide in the text a distinctive English name for every subspecies, these lengthy names are rarely used, the specific name being the obvious choice. Accordingly in this index only the specific vernacular names are given except in those cases where one subspecies has acquired a distinctive English name of its own. For example, twelve races of Canada Goose are illustrated on plate 5: in this index all are covered by the entry 'Canada Goose', but 'Cackling Goose' is also included, because this bird is not generally known as the 'Cackling Canada Goose'.

A few names not originally English have also been included, e.g., 'Ne-ne' for the Hawaiian Goose, familiarity being the criterion.

	Plate		Plate
Abyssinian Blue-winged Goose	7	Auckland Island Flightless Teal	10
African Black Duck	11	Auckland Island Merganser	22
African Maccoa Duck	23	Australian Blue-billed Duck	23
African Pochard	16	Australian Musk Duck	23
African Red-billed Pintail	9	Australian Pygmy Goose	18
African White-backed Duck	23	Australian Shelduck	6
Aleutian Teal	9	Australian Shoveler	12
American Black Duck	11	Australian White-eye	17
American Merganser	22		
American Wigeon	12		
Andaman Teal	10	Baer's Pochard	17
Andean Goose	7	Bahama Pintail (or *Duck*)	9
Andean Teal	9	Baikal Teal	10
Argentine Red Shoveler	12	*Baldpate* American Wigeon	12
Ashy-headed Goose	7	Bank's Island White-eye	17

	Plate		Plate
Bar-headed Goose	4	Bronze-winged Duck ..	9
Barnacle Goose	5	Bufflehead	21
Barrow's Goldeneye ..	21	*Burdekin Duck* Radjah	
Bean Goose	3	Shelduck	6
Bewick's Swan	2	*Butterball* Bufflehead ..	21
Birdikin Duck Radjah		*Butterball* Ruddy Duck ..	23
Shelduck	6		
Black Brant	5		
Black Duck..	11	Cackling Goose	5
'Black Geese'	5	Campbell Island Flightless	
Black Sheldrake New		Teal	10
Zealand Shelduck ..	6	Canada Goose	5
Black Scoter Common		Canvasback	16
Scoter	20	Cape Barren Goose ..	8
Black Swan	2	Cape Shelduck	6
Black Teal New Zealand		Cape Shoveler	12
Scaup	17	Cape Teal	9
Black-bellied Whistling Tree		Carolina	18
Duck Red-billed Whist-		Cereopsis Goose	8
ling Duck	1	Chestnut Teal	10
Black-billed Whistling		*Chestnut-breasted Teal*	
Duck	1	Chestnut Teal	10
Black-headed Duck ..	23	*Chile Teal* Chilian Teal ..	9
Black-necked Swan ..	2	Chilian Pintail	9
Blue Duck	13	Chilian Teal	9
Blue Goose	4	*Chilian Wigeon,* Chiloe	
Bluebill Scaup	17	Wigeon	12
Blue-billed Duck	23	Chiloe Wigeon	12
Blue-winged Goose ..	7	Chinese Merganser ..	22
Blue-winged Teal	12	Cinnamon Teal	12
Brahminy Duck Ruddy		*Clucking Teal* Formosa Teal	10
Shelduck	6	Comb Duck	19
Brazilian Teal	18	*Copper Teal* Cinnamon Teal	12
Brazilian Merganser ..	22	Coscoroba Swan	2
Brent Goose	5	*Cotton Teal* Indian Pygmy	
Broadbill Scaup	17	Goose	18
Brown Pintail Chilean		Coues's Gadwall	12
Pintail	9	Crested Duck	8
Brown Pochard South African		Crested Shelduck	6
or South American		*Crested Teal* Falcated Teal	10
Pochard	16	Crozet Pintail	9
Bronze-capped Duck		*Cuban Whistling Duck* Black-	
Falcated Teal	10	billed Whistling Duck ..	1

	Plate			Plate
Eaton's Pintail	9	Hawaiian Duck		11
Egyptian Goose	6	Hawaiian Goose		5
Eider	15	*Honker* Canada Goose ..		5
Emperor Goose	4	Hooded Merganser ..		22
European Wigeon	12	Hottentot Teal		9
Eyton's Tree Duck Plumed		*Hutchin's Goose* Richard-		
Whistling Duck	1	son's Goose		5
		Indian Pygmy Goose ..		18
Falcated Teal *or Duck* ..	10	Indian Whistling Duck ..		1
Ferruginous Duck ..	17			
Fischer's Eider	15	Jankowski's Swan		2
Flightless Steamer Duck ..	8	*Javan Tree or Whistling*		
Florida Duck	11	*Duck* Lesser Whistling		
Flying Steamer Duck ..	8	Duck		1
Formosa Teal	10			
Freckled Duck	13	Kelp Goose		7
Fulvous Whistling Duck ..	1	Kerguelen Pintail ..		9
		King Eider		15
Gadwall	12	*Knob-billed Duck* Comb		
Galapagos Pintail	9	Duck		19
Garganey	12	*Knob-nosed Goose* Comb		
Goldeneye	21	Duck		19
Goosander	22	*Koloa,* Hawaiian Duck ..		11
Greater Snow Goose ..	4			
Greater Whistling Teal ..		Labrador Duck		20
Fulvous Whistling Duck	1	Laysan Teal		11
Green Pygmy Goose ..	18	Lesser Scaup		17
Greenhead Mallard ..	11	Lesser Snow Goose ..		4
Green-winge Teal ..	9	Lesser Whistling Duck ..		1
Grey Duck (*Anas super-*		Lesser White-fronted Goose		3
ciliosa)	11	*Logger-headed Duck*		
Grey Duck Crested Duck ..	8	Steamer Duck		8
'Grey Geese'	3	Long-tailed Duck		21
Grey Teal (*Anas gibberi-*				
frons)	10	Maccoa Duck		23
Grey Teal (*Anas versicolor*)	9	Madagascar Teal		10
Greylag Goose	3	Madagascar White-backed		
		Duck		23
Harlequin Duck	21	Madagascar White-eye ..		17
Hartlaub's Duck *or Teal* ..	19			

89

Plate

Magellan Goose 7
Magpie Goose 1
Mallard 11
Mandarin Duck 18
Maned Goose Australian
  Wood Duck 18
Marbled Teal *or Duck* .. 9
Masked Duck 23
Meller's Duck 11
Merganet Torrent Duck .. 14
Merganser 22
Merida Teal 9
Mexican Duck 11
Monkey Duck Freckled
  Duck 13
Mountain Duck 13
Mountain Duck Australian
  Shelduck 6
Muscovy Duck 19
Musk Duck 23
Mute Swan 2

Ne-ne 5
New Zealand Brown Duck 10
New Zealand Scaup .. 17
New Zealand Shelduck .. 6
New Zealand Shoveler .. 12
Nile Goose Egyptian Goose 6
Niceforo's Pintail 9
North American Black
  Duck 11

Old Squaw 21
Orinoco Goose 6

Paradise Shelduck .. 6
Pepper Teal Silver Teal .. 9
Philippine Duck 11
Pink-eared Duck 13
Pink-footed Goose .. 3

Plate

Pink-headed Duck .. 13
Pintail 9
Plumed Whistling Duck .. 1
Pochard 16, 17
Polish Swan. (Colour phase
  of Mute Swan) 2
Puna Teal 9
Pygmy Goose 18

Radjah Shelduck 6
Red Shoveler 12
Red-billed Pintail *or Teal* 9
Red-billed Whistling Duck 1
Red-breasted Goose .. 5
Red-breasted Merganser .. 22
Red-crested Pochard .. 16
Redhead 16
Red-legged Black Duck
  North American Black
  Duck 11
Rice Teal Indian Pygmy
  Goose 18
Richardson's Goose .. 5
Ringbill Ring-necked Duck 17
Ringed Teal (*Ring-necked
  Teal*) 13
Ring-necked Duck.. .. 17
Ross's Goose 4
Rosybill 16
Ruddy Duck 23
Ruddy Shelduck 6
Ruddy-headed Goose .. 7

Salvadori's Duck 9
Scaly-sided Merganser
  Chinese Merganser .. 22
Scaup 17
Schuyl's Teal 18
Scoter 20
Sharp-winged Teal.. .. 9
Sheldrake Shelduck .. 6

90

	Plate
Sheldrake American Merganser	22
Shoveler	12
Silver Teal	9
Smew	22
Snow Goose	4
South African Pochard	16
South African Shelduck	6
South African Shoveler	12
South American Pochard	16
South Georgian Teal	9
Speckle-belly White-fronted Goose	3
Spectacled Eider	15
Spotbill	11
Spotted Whistling Duck	1
Sprig Pintail	9
Spur-winged Goose	19
Steamer Duck	8
Steller's Eider	15
Summer Teal Garganey	12
Surf Scoter	20
Sushkin's Goose. (Colour phase of Bean Goose)	3
Swan	2
Swan Goose	3
Teal	9, 10, 12, 13, 18
Torrent Duck	14
Tree Duck	1
Trumpeter Swan	2

	Plate
Tufted Duck	17
Tule Goose	3
Upland Goose	7
Velvet Scoter	20
Versicolor Teal Silver Teal	9
Wandering Whistling Duck	1
Wavey Snow Goose	4
Whistling Duck	1
Whistling Swan	2
White-backed Duck	23
White-eye	17
White-faced Whistling Duck	1
White-fronted Goose	3
White-headed Stifftail	23
White-winged Scoter	20
White-winged Wood Duck	19
Whooper Swan	2
Wigeon	12
Wild Duck, Mallard	11
Wood Duck, North American and Australian	18
Wood Duck, White-winged	19
Yellowbill	11
Yellow-billed Teal Chilean Teal	9

THE WILDFOWL TRUST

Slimbridge, Gloucestershire.	Telephone Cambridge (Glos.) 333
Peakirk, Northamptonshire.	Telephone Glinton 271
Caerlaverock, Dumfriesshire.	Telephone Glencaple 200
Welney, Cambridgeshire.	Telephone Littleport 711

Peter Scott founded the Wildfowl Trust in 1946, to study ducks, geese and swans, and to find and put into action ways of assessing and conserving their populations. Increasing pressures on wildfowl and the wetlands where they live underline the continuing importance of this work, which depends for funds largely on voluntary support.

The site which he chose, near Slimbridge on the east bank of the Severn Estuary, was already a famous resort of wildfowl; now it is the home of the largest and most varied collection of living wildfowl in the world, and a research centre of world renown whose activities cover all aspects of wildfowl and wetlands conservation at an international as well as national level.

In winter large numbers of wild birds come to Slimbridge, encouraged by the protection which we give to them and their feeding grounds. The Dumbles, an area of saltings on the river bank, is the winter home of a flock of up to 6,000 wild White-fronted Geese and as many as 400 wild Bewick's Swans may come to feed during a day on Swan Lake in front of the Trust's buildings. An attraction throughout the year at Slimbridge is the Tropical House, in which species of wildfowl too delicate to survive our winters are provided with a suitable home, shared by tanagers and humming birds which nest in the lush vegetation. Slimbridge is famous too for its breeding flocks of flamingos. Now that the area of the New Grounds is to be increased, there are plans for a Temperate House to complement the Tropical House, and a Rotunda with heated quarters for other less hardy birds. A special wood has been set aside for tree ducks, where they will be able to fly free and nest in their natural habitat.

A second establishment, at Peakirk in Northamptonshire, is only slightly smaller than that at Slimbridge. Both are open to the public throughout the year.

CONSERVATION

One result of the work of the Trust has been the development of a national network of wildfowl refuges, some of them controlled by us. The land is managed for the well-being of the birds, using methods discovered and developed by the Trust. In our refuges, at Caerlaverock on the Solway and at Welney on the Ouse Washes as well as at Slimbridge, systems of observation hides and screening banks permit people to obtain very close views of wild geese and ducks, as well as other species which take advantage of the protection which we afford.

In the collections visitors can study and photograph the birds at close quarters. Many of the birds will feed confidently from the hand, and as many as possible are left full-winged and free to fly. This chance to see and enjoy the birds without undue difficulty introduces many people who might never have looked at birds before to a whole new field of recreation.

The Trust's success in breeding rare species is of particular value. The Hawaiian Goose, or Ne-ne, is a case in point: at one time there were

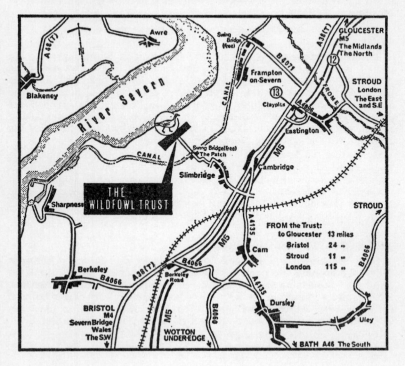

93

only 32 of these birds left in the world but by 1971 665 had been bred at Slimbridge, and 200 had been flown back to the island of Maui to re-establish the species in the wild. Similar projects are now under way with the White-winged Wood Duck from Assam, and several other species.

RESEARCH

The Research Unit at Slimbridge, under the direction of Professor Geoffrey Matthews, enjoys an international reputation. As well as working on all aspects of the biology of wildfowl, the unit houses the International Waterfowl Research Bureau, and is the centre of a large and complex counting system for mapping and monitoring wildfowl populations. The Trust operates a ringing scheme based on the 17th century duck decoy at Borough Fen near Peakirk, and on Berkeley New Decoy at Slimbridge and other trapping stations.

The flock of Bewick's Swans which comes to the Trust from Siberia each winter has become the subject of a unique enquiry into the family life of migrant wildfowl. Each swan has a distinctive individual face-pattern: about 1,400 have been named at Slimbridge, and can be recognized when they return to our sanctuary. Other intensive research is discovering the habitat preferences and diet of wild geese and ducks, with a view to improving the lot of the large numbers of migrants which come to Britain each winter.

All facets of the Unit's work are illustrated in a permanent exhibition on show at Slimbridge.

EDUCATION

25,000 children each year from 600 schools visit Slimbridge, making use of the full-time education service which the Trust provides. The preparatory material includes sets of slides, film strips, and teaching notes; during their visit the children use worksheets which direct their attention to crucial questions of ecology and biology. As much effort goes into the education of adults, by means of lectures, exhibitions, and film shows, away from the Trust. The aim of this work, like that of the research, is to advance the cause of conservation.

By visiting the Trust's collections and refuges you can help to support the work which we have undertaken; by becoming a member you will not only help us financially but also give us the increased moral support which we need to make our voice even more clearly heard in the planning councils. The details of the various types of membership can be obtained from The Secretary, The Wildfowl Trust, Slimbridge, Glos.

ARRANGEMENTS FOR VISITORS

Both **Slimbridge** and **Peakirk** are open every day (except Christmas Day); the grounds are open at 9.30 a.m. on weekdays and 12 noon on Sundays, Sunday mornings being reserved for members and their friends. Visitors are admitted up to 5.30 p.m. when sunset is later than 6.00 p.m. or up to half an hour before sunset when it is earlier. Visitors may stay in the grounds for up to one hour after the latest time for admission.

At **Welney** and **Caerlaverock** (Eastpark Farm) visits are strictly controlled, to avoid disturbance to the birds. The size of parties is limited,

94

and intending visitors are advised to apply well in advance to the Warden.

The charges for admission to the various establishments may be obtained from any Wildfowl Trust refuge.

YOUTH HOSTELS

There is a Youth Hostel at Slimbridge, especially designed and built for use as a field study centre. It has two well-equipped workrooms, a photographic darkroom, and a good naturalists' library including maps of the area. The Hostels may be booked by school parties who wish to work at the Trust: enquiries should be addressed in the first instance to The Warden, The Youth Hostel, Shepherd's Patch, Slimbridge.

Other Trust establishments are not so well placed for hostelling: the nearest hostel to Peakirk and Welney is at King's Lynn, about 20 miles away; and the closest to Eastpark Farm are Carlisle in England and Kenoon in Scotland. Information about the Trust refuges is available at all these hostels.

FUTURE DEVELOPMENTS

The need for the Trust's work is increasing all the time, and with it the opportunity for spreading our message. New collections with wild refuges alongside are being planned in other parts of the country. These plans have reached an advanced stage at Arundel in Sussex, centred on water meadows below the castle, and at Martin Mere in Lancashire, where the

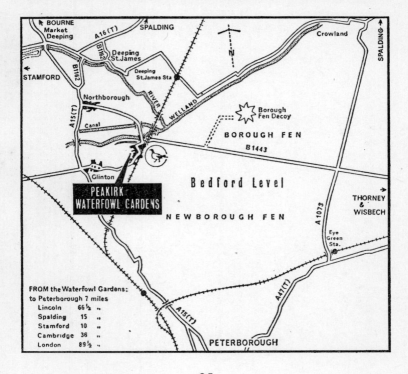

ancient lake, long since drained, is to be re-excavated and made once more into a haunt of water birds. In both these places collections similar to that at Slimbridge will be opened to the public, for their recreation and education.

Other sites are also under consideration, but all these plans must lie dormant until money is available to carry them out. An immediate need is for money to perfect the grounds at Slimbridge itself, where more land is at last available adjoining the present site. A special fund-raising campaign has been launched to collect the money for all these works: any contributions are welcome, but most especially Deeds of Covenant, which enable the Trust to benefit from its status as a registered charity.

SLIMBRIDGE
January, 1972

NOTES